CURSE
of the
CANNIBALS

Virgil E. Robinson

TEACH Services, Inc.
P U B L I S H I N G
www.TEACHServices.com

Facsimile Reproduction

This book played a formative role in the development of Christian thought and the publisher feels that this book, with its candor and depth, still holds significance for the church today. Therefore the publisher has chosen to reproduce this historical classic from an original copy. Frequent variations in the quality of the print are unavoidable due to the condition of the original. Thus the print may look darker or lighter or appear to be missing detail, more in some places than in others.

Copyright © 2005 TEACH Services, Inc.
ISBN-13: 978-1-57258-355-9
Library of Congress Control Number: 2005934295

Published by

TEACH Services, Inc.
P U B L I S H I N G
www.TEACHServices.com

CONTENTS

BOYHOOD DAYS

"JOHNNIE-E-E! Johnnie-e-e!"

Mrs. Paton's call rang out on the clear afternoon air and echoed back from the hill across the valley. There was no reply, but a shepherd on a nearby road, charmed by the lovely voice, turned and looked.

Father Paton stepped out the front door of his Scottish home. It was a long low building with a steep, thatched roof. At one end was the large room in which the family lived, and at the other end was an equally large room in which the father carried on his home factory for knitting stockings. Between the two rooms, like the filling of a sandwich, was the closet which the Paton children called the sanctuary. It was to this room that Father Paton retired three times a day to pour out his heart to God. No one ever disturbed him there.

Now he walked up to where his wife stood, scanning the distant hillside.

"What's the matter?" asked Mr. Paton sympathetically. "Is John lost?"

"He may not be lost, but I wonder where he can be. He left this morning to go rambling in the hills, but he has never stayed away so long before."

"Just remember he is growing up. An eight-year-old is sure to wander farther and stay away longer than a six-year-old. Besides, there is nothing that can hurt him. Did he take any lunch?"

"I thought he might get hungry, so I gave him a bit of bread and cheese."

"Don't worry then. These hikes are good for him. They toughen him up."

Mrs. Paton went back into the kitchen to care for her other three children. As the sun neared the horizon the anxious mother, watching from a window, saw John's childish figure climbing the hill. With a sigh of relief she stepped out to greet her eldest child.

"John, John, wherever have you been? Why did you stay so long? Look, you have torn your pants."

Johnnie looked down sadly at his torn trouser leg.

"I'm sorry, Mamma. But I had the best time today! I followed the water up the glen, and see what I found!"

He pulled three snowy-white stones out of his pocket and displayed them proudly.

"Well, come in now and wash up. It's nearly time for tea."

Every day found Father Paton toiling at his work. Although he had no difficulty selling his stockings in nearby towns, the price he received was so low that it was hard for him to make ends meet. The small garden patch was not fertile, and much patient work was needed to make the vegetables grow. Then the children had come so fast; first John, then Peter, then other boys and girls until eventually they numbered eleven! At times it seemed the small house must burst its walls. However, by the time the last child was born, John had already left the family nest.

Life in the Paton home followed a regular pattern. Every Sunday morning the father led his children over the hills to Dumfries to worship in the small church there, then walked home with them after the service. The mother was no less pious than the father, but she was not strong enough for the eight-mile hike, so she seldom attended.

From the age of seven John attended the Thorowold

school, where the teacher spent more time teaching Bible than arithmetic. Father would gladly have invited John into the shop to help with the loom, but when he saw how eager his son was to learn, he willingly let him go to school.

"I wish it were possible to put you into a better suit of clothes," remarked the father one morning as John, with slate in one hand and lunch pail in the other, was leaving for another day of school. " 'Tis plain enough you come from a poor family," he remarked sorrowfully.

"Never mind, Father," John said cheerfully. "Other boys are just as poor as I am. Why not pray for some better clothes? Perhaps God will send them to us."

John began to pray. Every day for a month he asked the Lord for the clothes he needed, and he did not become discouraged when his prayers were not immediately answered.

John was an extremely bright student, and soon became a favorite with the schoolteacher, who was pleased with the lad's eagerness to learn. John's threadbare clothing did not escape the teacher's notice.

One evening as the Patons were kneeling in prayer, the children's quick ears heard a faint click as the door opened, then closed softly. Immediately after the amen, John rushed to see what the opening of the door had meant. On the floor he found a neatly tied parcel. Inside was a fine new suit of warm clothes. John's faith had been rewarded. With a smile he said to his mother, "God sent them, I know!"

"Yes, dear," she replied, thankful to see his growing faith.

The next morning John proudly wore his new suit to school and eagerly told the teacher about the mysterious visit of an unknown stranger. The lad failed to notice the smile on the teacher's face.

"John," he told the boy, "whenever you need anything after this, just tell your father to read the Book, and God will send what you need in answer to his prayer." Many years later John discovered that the timely gift had come from the schoolteacher himself.

Although gifted with a warm heart, the teacher was cursed with a violent temper. Schools in those days were ruled by the rod, and boys received many floggings when their lessons were not learned as perfectly as the teacher demanded. On some days it seemed that the least trifle would throw John's teacher into a rage.

John stood at the head of his class. One October day the teacher offered a prize of ten shillings to the scholar who by Christmas would turn in the best Latin composition. John spent long hours copying and recopying his work. His finished product was the best composition submitted in the judgment of another teacher. His own teacher, however, gave the prize to the son of the wealthiest man in the parish, although his theme was not as good as John's. John didn't like that, and for a while he did not try as hard as before.

One morning the teacher discovered on his desk a box bearing the words "With the compliments of John Paton." Thinking it must be some valuable present, he lifted the lid. To his dismay a large rat leaped out onto the desk, dropped to the floor, and scurried out of the door. Of course John had nothing to do with the trick. But the enraged teacher gave him no time to explain. Seizing the boy by the arm, he dragged him to his desk and flogged him severely.

At home John told his parents what had happened. Although his desire for an education was as strong as ever, he was determined never to return to that school. Unable, however, to resist his mother's pleading, he consented to return the following morning. It was a troubled lad who tossed on his bunk that night.

Next morning, wondering how the teacher would receive him, John walked hesitantly down the road. When the teacher saw the boys crossing the schoolyard, he rushed out of the building, ran straight at John, and kicked him violently. The boy turned and fled. This time nothing could persuade him to return to the classroom. Not even the pleadings of the teacher himself could induce him to change his mind.

The teacher opened the box, and a big rat jumped out.

John now joined his father in the shop, where they worked together from six each morning till ten at night, with only a half hour off for breakfast and supper, and an hour for lunch. Each day John used some of those free minutes to study his books.

Father Paton was an earnest Christian. He rejoiced as he saw his children choosing to follow Jesus. Every morning at family worship the young ones would hear their father pray that God would send missionaries to teach the heathen in faraway lands. John was so deeply impressed that he decided to give his life in service to God.

When John was only fifteen years old the potato crop failed. Food prices soared. Father Paton left work one morning with a bundle of stockings for customers in the city of Hawick, fully expecting to return the next evening with money and supplies. He was unaware of the food situation at home when he left. In the kitchen Mother Paton looked anxiously at bare cupboards. That evening as she set the last bite of food on the table, she told her children there was no more, but that she had asked God to send them some breakfast. They went to sleep eager to see how God would answer that prayer.

Morning came, but still there was nothing to put on the table. The children watched the road. Around ten o'clock they saw a man from the town of Lockerbie coming up the path carrying a large parcel, which he handed to Mrs. Paton. With tear-filled eyes she read the note accompanying the parcel. The note explained that her own father had felt moved to send them a love offering and hoped they could use it. The parcel contained a bag of new potatoes, fourteen pounds of flour, and the first homemade cheese of the season. Turning to her family, Mrs. Paton said, "Children, love your heavenly Father; tell Him in faith and prayer all your needs, and He will supply them." Never again did the family fortunes drop so low as on that occasion.

When John had saved a few shillings he enrolled at the nearby Dumfries academy for a six-week course. His love for learning was rekindled, and he determined to find a job that would pay enough so he could go to school.

A few days later he was employed by a surveying company. Because his workday ended at four in the afternoon, he had plenty of time for study. While his companions played soccer and other games, John found some quiet corner and studied. The company manager noticed this, and talked with the young man. John told of his longing for an education. The following Monday he was called in before the manager.

"Master Paton," said the man, "we respect you for your love of learning. I have been authorized to send you to Woolwich for an intensive course at government expense. All you need to do is sign this paper promising to serve for seven years when your course is finished."

"I'm sorry, sir, but I cannot do it. For three or four years I might, but for seven, no."

"Pray tell, why not? Do you realize that the sons of gentlemen would be proud and happy to accept such an offer?"

"My life is given to another Master," John replied, "so I cannot engage myself for seven years."

"To whom?"

"To the Lord Jesus, and I want to prepare as soon as possible for His service in proclaiming the gospel."

The man leaped to his feet in a rage.

"Accept my offer, or you are dismissed on the spot!"

Politely but firmly John declined again. He was paid off and sent away. A week later he accepted work on a farm, where he stayed all summer. It was hard work, but the farmer's wife was kind to him. In his spare time he studied. At her suggestion he shared a room in the big house with the farmer's own son. He repaid her kindness by planting a beautiful flower garden in front of the house.

One day while reading a Christian paper from Glasgow, John saw a notice that aroused his interest. A man was needed to work for the poor in that large city. The Reformed

Presbyterian Church would pay fifty pounds a year to a suitable person.

John wrote at once, offering his services. Eventually he received a letter from Dr. Bates, the minister at the mission, inviting him to Glasgow for an interview.

Having finished his farm work, John returned home and told his parents of his plans to work for God in Glasgow. They were pleased, even though John would be leaving home. At that time there was no train from Dumfries to Glasgow and the stagecoach was too expensive. So John decided to walk the sixty miles. His belongings fitted into a very small bundle. They consisted of his Bible, one change of clothing, and a handkerchief.

On the morning of John's departure, Father Paton decided to accompany his son to a point some six miles along the road. They walked in silence, side by side, each busy with his thoughts. At length they reached the place where they were to part. Halting, Father Paton grasped his son's hand and exclaimed with deep emotion, "God bless you, my son! May your father's God protect you, and keep you from all evil."

After a farewell embrace they separated. John walked rapidly along the road toward Glasgow. At a bend in the road he looked back and saw his father still standing at the spot where they had parted, his head uncovered, his face lifted heavenward. With tears in his eyes, John rounded the corner and walked on for a few minutes. Longing to see his father once more, he climbed the dike running parallel to the road, only to see his father also climbing the dike back where he had been standing. The old man did not see him, and after a few moments, they both descended to the road and continued on their respective journeys.

John spent the two nights of his journey at the homes of kind farmers. In Glasgow he found a cheap room where he could sleep, but he would have to feed himself. Next morning at the mission hall he met another young man who had also come to apply for the position. The tests were oral. Dr.

Bates asked the questions. At the end of the examination the doctor consulted with his associates, then spoke to the eager young men.

"We find it impossible to decide; you both did well in the examinations. But we have only fifty pounds. Is there any possibility that you might live together, share expenses, and divide the fifty pounds between you? If you can accept this arrangement, the society will pay your entrance fees to the Free Normal Seminary."

John and the other candidate agreed to try it. They found a large room and boarded themselves while doing their work and attending school part of the day. Unfortunately, they did not eat properly. Before that winter was over, both fell sick. They had to quit their work and leave Glasgow. John returned home to a real welcome. Good food and loving care soon restored him to health.

Hoping to save some money and thus make it possible to finish his education, John taught school that winter. Out of his rather small salary he managed to save ten pounds, which he took with him back to Glasgow where he enrolled in the college again. But expenses were heavier than he had expected, and within a few months he was down to his last penny. He wrote a few lines to his parents, describing his sad experience. He expected to leave Glasgow, he told them, and find work somewhere else. He would write again after he had found a suitable job.

With this letter in his pocket he went out, carrying his few books in a basket, hoping to find someone willing to buy them so that he would have money to buy food for a few days. He hesitated at the door of a pawnbroker's shop, wondering if the owner would have any earthly use for such books as his. Most likely the man would not even buy them. Then, glancing across the street, he saw a notice in a store window.

"Teacher wanted. Maryhill Free Church School. Apply at the Manse."

A coach happened to be passing. Without a moment's

hesitation John leaped aboard, handed the driver his last penny, and rode to the house of the minister. He was hired and was given ten shillings in advance. Returning to his room he paid his landlady and tore up the letter he had written to his parents. Then he wrote another letter, full of good news and encouraging words, telling of his new job.

The minister who had hired John warned him that the school was a wreck owing to the bad behavior of the children. When the two of them visited the school the minister showed John a thick heavy cane in the desk and warned him, "Unless you use this freely, you will never keep order here!"

John took the instrument from the hands of the minister, felt it for a moment, then replaced it in the desk.

"That will be my last resort."

"I don't think you realize that seven teachers have been run out of this school," the minister told him.

John soon found that he was operating two schools. One met in the morning with an enrollment of eighteen, the other at night with twenty scholars. It was not long before a bully sought to break up the school. John ordered him to keep quiet or leave the room. The fellow laughed at the young teacher. Rolling up his sleeves, he dared John to fight him.

The teacher picked up the cane and advanced toward his unruly pupil. Although the boy tried to fight back, the cane was too much for him, and after many blows he staggered to his seat where he sat in sulky silence.

The cane was returned to the desk and was never used again. Boys who were bent on mischief stayed away and the others made good progress. The number of scholars increased steadily, and the school lost its bad reputation.

The trustees were very pleased to have so many paying pupils, but one day the chairman came to see John. "Mr. Paton," he began, "we have found another teacher. We like you, the children like you, but this man is more highly qualified than you are."

16

John was stunned, for the blow was so unexpected. Word quickly spread among the parents that a new teacher was coming to take over. Many of them felt bad when they heard about it. Some even got up a petition asking that John remain, but it did no good. Once again he was out of a job. Would he ever be able to complete his education?

"What next?" murmured the young man. "If ever there was a rolling stone, I am sure its name was John Paton!"

SEARCHING FOR JEWELS

JOHN sat on the edge of his bed, wondering what to do. He had just finished his last day of teaching at Maryhill School. It was unfair, the way the school board had treated him. He had accepted the teaching job when no one else would, he had doubled the school's enrollment, and he had made the school one of the best in the city.

Unemployed! Yes, that's what I am! John groaned to himself. My rent is due next week. How can I pay it if I don't have a job?

It was not natural for John to be discouraged. After eating a simple supper he picked up his Bible, hoping to find a comforting passage for his wounded soul. In the forty-first chapter of Isaiah he read the words, "Fear thou not; for I am with thee: be not dismayed; for I am thy God." A great burden rolled off his heart. He knelt by his bed.

"Thank You, Lord, thank You for that promise. I believe it with all my heart. Perhaps tomorrow You will show me what to do."

John's faith was not disappointed. After breakfast, as he was preparing to go across the city to interview a Christian businessman he knew in the hope of obtaining work, he heard a rap on the door. A young stranger stood outside, holding a long envelope, which bore the return address of the Glasgow City Mission. John tore it open and read:

"Dear Mr. Paton,

"You will remember that about a year ago, shortly before you took the Maryhill school, you applied for work with our organization. We are well aware of all that you did for that school. I now invite you to join us in our work. If you feel that God is leading you in this direction, kindly come to our office tomorrow morning. Our directors would like to meet you.

"Sincerely,
Thomas Caie"

For a moment John stood amazed. He thought of Eliezer, Abraham's servant, whose prayer had been answered almost before he finished making it.

"Any reply?" asked the messenger.

"Why, yes, of course. Please tell Mr. Caie that I will be there at nine."

The next morning Paton knocked on the door of the director of the Glasgow City Mission. A short interview followed. The gentlemen gathered in the room were greatly surprised by John's wide knowledge of the Bible. Mr. Caie explained the next step.

"Mr. Paton, so far you have done very well. Now we have a practical test for you."

"I'll be glad to do whatever I can," John replied. "I believe you have the kind of work I am eager to enter."

"Very well. Two of our directors will accompany you tomorrow morning into the slum area of this city. You will visit the people in their homes, speaking to them about Jesus and inviting them to follow Him. Finally, on Sunday, you will hold a meeting in the mission district and the directors will listen to your sermon."

Not knowing just what he might be getting into, Paton kept his appointment the next morning. For two hours he climbed stairs and entered hovels and damp basements in search of souls who needed help. In one house he found a sick child; in another a mother was ill. He found families living in cold, dark cellars. He found children whose feet had been bitten by rats. Many tenements had no heat for either cooking or warmth.

He talked with these people, read parts of the Bible to them, and told them of the One who cares. He told stories to the children. He jotted down one address where the family was completely without food, and promised that help would be sent. He urged heavy drinkers to give up their bad habit. In one room he asked an old woman dying of consumption whether she was a Christian. Her eyes lighted up.

"Oh, yes, I know Jesus," she whispered. John prayed for her. His eyes filled with tears as he looked at her bedding which was only a bundle of rags. As he left, he wondered whether he would see her again.

The next Sunday morning Mr. Paton preached in the chapel. It was crowded, and he was happy to recognize one or two people whom he had visited.

Three days later he was told that the members of the board were satisfied. From henceforth he would be a member of the team of the Glasgow City Mission, with a salary of forty pounds a year. He was given a marked map showing the city areas in which he was to work.

John immediately set about visiting every home in his district, no matter how wretched it was. In some houses he was told that no Christian worker had called for ten or more years. Many of the men were atheists. They did not believe in God at all. Nearly every street had its saloons, or public houses, as they were called in Scotland. John realized how much grief was caused by the liquor so plentifully available everywhere.

As he went over his parish, Paton looked for a place where he might hold public services. Open-air meetings might be all right in summer, but in winter it would be necessary to have shelter. He mentioned this problem to a Christian shopkeeper. She was far from wealthy, but she did have a small room that she told Paton he could use for evening services. He secured the use of a haymow in the second floor of a barn for his Sunday morning services.

The shopkeeper warned John, "You'll have to watch out for my husband. He doesn't like preachers. But he never gets home from the public house before midnight, so I think you'll be all right." Later John learned that this man often beat his wife and forced her to give him money to buy drink.

Great was Paton's surprise when the husband of the shopkeeper walked into one of his evening meetings. He liked what he heard and came back again. Finally he gave up his drink, was baptized, and became a strong Christian.

Still the work went hard. At the end of his first year, Paton had to report that only seven persons were attending services regularly. One day the mission director sent for him.

"Mr. Paton," he began, "we know that your assigned area is one of the most difficult in Glasgow. We admire the way you have gone about your work. As we expected, results have been small. Since we do not want you to become discouraged, we are moving you to a better district."

Suddenly Paton felt very sad. True, the fruit had been small, but it was very precious to his heart. He loved every one of his converts. The thought of leaving was more than he could endure.

"Mr. Caie, I thank you for your kind words," he said. "It is not for us to say which soil will bear a rich harvest. Our duty is to sow the seed. Please don't take me away from my district. Give me six more months. It has taken time to gain the confidence of the people. I want you to pray for them."

At his next service Paton announced that the directors wanted to move him to another district.

One man sprang to his feet, declaring, "Mr. Paton, they mustn't do that. I know we are few in number, but I am sure we can bring more." He turned to the others present.

"Who will pledge with me to bring someone with him to the next meeting?" Every hand went up.

That was the turning point. At the next meeting there were fifteen, and the following month the attendance doubled again. A Bible class was started, then a singing class. Finally Paton launched a Total Abstinence Society, whose members promised never again to touch a drop of liquor. The old barn could no longer hold the congregation. Paton looked around for a larger place. After praying earnestly for guidance he felt impressed to visit a friend, Mr. Binnie. This Christian man bought a good plot of ground and built a mission hall on it, all at his own expense.

Every Sunday morning at seven nearly a hundred young people attended a Bible study class. Most of them wore work clothing; they had nothing better. Several were even barefooted. Before the end of three years the chapel, built to seat six hundred, was packed every Sunday. Paton's influence spread all over that part of Glasgow. Scores of men and women, boys and girls, signed the pledge.

Naturally the saloonkeepers became very angry when fewer customers visited their shops. They determined to try to stop the meetings which were then being held in a hall in Thomson's Lane, a short, wide street not open for traffic. First they laid a complaint against Paton at the local police station. They stated that owing to his work their trade was being ruined. They were taxpayers, they pointed out, and their businesses should be protected.

They did not know that the police captain and Paton were good friends. The captain was most grateful as he saw crime and drunkenness lessening in his district. But hiding his true feelings, he promised the saloonkeepers that some policemen would attend John's next meeting. The men left with a wrong impression of the captain's true feelings.

The saloonkeepers and a number of their friends were present at Paton's next meeting. They hoped to witness the breakup of the gathering. Just as the service was starting, a body of police approached and took up positions in various places. The publicans winked at their friends and waited to see what would happen.

Suddenly the captain himself pushed his way through the crowd, walked up onto the platform, and sat down beside Mr. Paton. The saloonkeepers dared not leave, since they had requested the police themselves. At the close of Mr. Paton's address the captain got up and made a speech. He enthusiastically endorsed all that the preacher had said about the evils of strong drink!

The saloonkeepers tried another trick. One day during a meeting, a heavy van was driven up directly in front of the gate and left there. After church the members could not leave because the opening was blocked. Mr. Paton directed two young men to crawl under the wagon and pull it out of the way. As they were doing this, they were arrested by two policemen who had been hiding nearby. John followed them. He soon caught up and asked, "Why are you taking these young men away?"

"They are under arrest for disturbing private property."

"But they were simply moving the van so that people could leave church. They did no damage to it."

The policemen said, "You had better leave, or you will be arrested also."

But John said, "I am going with you to the police station."

When they arrived an officer wrote out the particulars of the case. Mr. Paton tried to explain what had happened, but the police would not listen.

The young men were about to be taken to prison cells when a well-dressed gentleman entered.

"What bail is required?" he asked.

The officer mumbled an answer.

"I know all about this case and I know who is behind this arrest," the man said. "If there is a trial on Monday morning, I shall be here to expose the whole dirty business." Then he walked out.

Deliberately the officer at the desk arose and tore up the paper containing the charge.

"You are free to leave," he said. "I regret the inconvenience this has caused you."

From that time on the saloonkeepers decided it was best

"If there is a trial on Monday morning, I shall be here to expose the whole dirty business."

to leave Mr. Paton and his temperance people alone.

One day a well-dressed woman visited John at the mission. After introducing herself, she said, "I have a sad story to tell you, Mr. Paton. My nephew is one of the best doctors in Glasgow. He has a lovely wife and two beautiful children who have learned to flee at the sight of him when he is drunk. He has made his home a hell for his wife and children. He is on his way to a drunkard's grave. Oh, won't you please visit him and see if you can do anything?"

Out of pity for the family, Paton agreed. He had a conversation with the doctor. They talked for several hours. Then, after reading some passages from the Bible, Paton suggested prayer.

The man was deeply impressed by Paton's words.

"Yes, by all means, pray," he said.

"But you must pray for yourself."

"Pray, I cannot pray. I can curse, but I cannot pray."

"When I came, did you not agree to listen and do what I asked?"

"Yes, but you are asking the impossible!"

"Just try to pray," begged Paton, "and then we will both know whether you can or not."

For a moment there was silence. Then the man burst forth, "O Lord, Thou knowest I cannot pray." He would have gone on, perhaps to say something blasphemous, but Paton lifted his voice in prayer, pleading with God for that family. The man was deeply moved.

"Now I have one request to make before I leave," said Paton.

"What is that?"

"You need rest. Promise me you will lie down and take a good sleep." The man agreed.

That evening, when his classes were over, Paton visited the home again. The doctor met him at the door, clasped his hands, and exclaimed, "Thank God, I can pray now."

Not all the people Mr. Paton visited yielded their hearts to God. Some on the brink of death stopped their ears, turned their faces to the wall and died. But hundreds were converted and found peace in following Jesus.

There was no more talk of transferring Paton to another district. The boys and girls who worked in the Glasgow mills loved him as a father. He was known everywhere, and in many of the homes he visited he was regarded as an angel of mercy.

Ten years passed, every one of them filled with soul-rewarding work for John Paton. One might think he had every reason to be satisfied and willing to remain the rest of his life in city mission work. But he could never forget the prayers of his godly father on behalf of the heathen that were perishing in total darkness, and their appeals for help. Many times he wondered where his duty lay.

One day John heard that the mission he had worked for when he first arrived in Glasgow ten years before was looking for someone to go as a missionary to the islands of the South Pacific. Dr. Bates, the man who had first employed him, wept for joy at finding a volunteer.

"Will you go to the New Hebrides?" asked Dr. Bates.

"I will go wherever I am most needed," said Mr. Paton.

Strange as it may seem, when that night Paton told Joseph Copeland, his roommate, about his decision, the young man decided that he too would go to the South Seas.

But what will father and mother think of my going so far from home, particularly to such a dangerous area? wondered John. He explained his desires in a long letter home. To his great joy both of his parents replied that they had given him, their firstborn son, to the Lord when he was born, and would rejoice to see him go to a foreign land.

Paton was surprised to discover how many people were strongly opposed to his going to the New Hebrides. When his parishioners heard of it they wept and begged him not to leave them. The directors of the Glasgow City Mission promised not to stand in his way, but begged him to find someone to take his place. His mind turned to his brother, Walter, an earnest Christian businessman in a nearby city.

At his suggestion Mr. Caie wrote to Walter, inviting him to Glasgow. Walter gladly responded. It was a happy day for Paton when he could take his brother around and introduce him to his many friends and converts.

One dear old Christian protested to Paton several times.

"You'll be eaten by cannibals! You will be eaten by cannibals!"

Weary of his many protests, Paton finally answered in these words: "You see, Mr. Dickson, you are an old man and must die sometime. Then the worms will eat you. Suppose I go to the South Sea Islands and the cannibals eat me. We both get eaten in any case. Will it be any worse for me to be eaten by cannibals than for you to be eaten by worms? Won't we both come forth at the same resurrection?"

"After that, I have nothing more to say," exclaimed the old man, throwing up his hands in dismay.

Paton had a secret which he had not shared with the director of the mission board. A young lady, Janet Ann Robson, had for some time been of real assistance to him in the mission hall. She was talented and worthy of Paton's growing love for her. Instead of being frightened when she learned of his plan to go to the cannibal islands, she gloried in the thought of going with him. After she had accepted his proposal they both agreed that the mission board would have to be told. Paton would need a little larger salary, and perhaps even a larger cabin on the vessel that would take them halfway round the world.

But before they had time to break the news to the chairman of the board he sent for John. Dr. Bates quickly introduced the subject that was uppermost in his mind.

"Mr. Paton, you can't go to the mission field single. It just isn't done. Who will cook your food and take care of your clothes? Also you will need someone to keep you company out there among the savages. Don't you think it might be possible to find a young woman willing to marry you and go to the mission field with you and be your helper and companion?"

Paton nearly laughed out loud. Before he could answer, Dr. Bates read his secret on his face. Clapping his hands together joyfully, he exclaimed, "You've got her, John! I can see it on your face!"

"Yes, I have a treasure, and she's as happy as I am to be going to the mission field."

"Wonderful! That's all settled then. Surely the Lord is good."

"Amen," whispered Paton softly.

A DARK LAND

DECEMBER 25, 1857, was one Christmas Day John Paton would never forget. At the hour of three that afternoon, in a Presbyterian church in one of the suburbs of Glasgow, the missionary appointee and Janet Ann Robson became husband and wife.

"What are your plans, Mr. Paton?" asked Mr. Robson after the ceremony. "How long will you and Janet be with us?"

"The mission society has asked me to visit all the churches of the Reformed Group," John replied, "and get their promise to help support our island mission."

"Do you plan to take Janet with you?"

A little startled at the thought of being separated from his bride of only a few hours, John asked, "Why not? For many months I have looked forward to the time when we could be together all the time."

"Well, son, have you thought what it will mean to her mother and to me when you take her to the other side of the world? For the sake of her mother, who is dreading the parting so soon to come, please allow Janet to remain at home while you make this tour."

"Father Robson, you and mother have my sympathy. But I would not wish to make such a decision without consulting Janet. I will let you know what she says."

The next morning John informed Mr. Robson and his wife that Janet would remain with them while he traveled.

Paton was well received by the churches of Scotland, but before he had finished visiting all of them the time came to prepare to sail. Returning to Glasgow he rejoined his wife. Then on March 23, 1858, John Paton was ordained to the gospel ministry and set apart as a missionary to the New Hebrides.

The next four weeks were busy ones for the missionary appointees as they purchased articles that would be unobtainable in the far-off islands. Each day it seemed there was another box to be nailed up. One afternoon a large wagon drew up in front of the Robson home. On the back, perched on a large box, sat one of Paton's Sunday school superintendents from the Glasgow Mission. The man pushed the box to the edge of the wagon, then jumped to the ground.

"Put this with your other boxes, Mrs. Paton," he said, easing it off the wagon.

"What's in it?"

"Wouldn't you rather wait and open it at your new home? Then you'll have a surprise."

John smiled.

"No, I think we might as well know now. Perhaps it is something we won't need to take," he teased, a twinkle in his eye.

"Well, then, if you must know, your boys and girls from the mills saved up a bit of money, then used it to buy calico print. In this box you will find fifty dresses for the heathen women, and fifty pairs of pants for the men."

Paton's eyes filled with tears.

"God bless the noble lads and lassies! Tell them I will never forget them."

"What's more, Mr. Paton," added the man, "they plan to send a similar box every year you stay out there."

The day came for the missionaries to leave. On the Glasgow docks the last farewells took place as the Patons and Joseph Copeland boarded the sailing ship *Clutha,* bound for Melbourne, Australia. Friends and relatives watched with tear-dimmed eyes as the vessel sailed with the tide. There was no furlough policy in those days and the Robsons and Patons had no idea when they would see their beautiful daughter and brave son again.

The voyage was pleasant, but tiresome. When the wind blew, the ship skimmed over the water, but many times the wind died away, and they were becalmed. It was very hot in the tropics. One important stop was made at Cape Town where fresh water, fruits, and vegetables were taken on board. The Patons enjoyed walking on dry land again after more than seven weeks on the *Clutha.*

The trip from Cape Town to Melbourne was very tedious also. The captain did all he could to make the voyage pleasant. At his request, Mr. Paton held Bible classes regularly with the crew and passengers. Mrs. Paton played games with Jessie and Donald Wilson, two children placed in their care who were journeying from England to Australia to rejoin their parents. At Melbourne, the Patons went to hand over the children and relax for a few days while Mr. Copeland stayed on the ship caring for the baggage and looking for a ship that would take them to the New Hebrides. Finally he heard of an American ship, the *Frances P. Sage,* en route to Penang. The captain agreed to take the Patons, Mr. Copeland, and their fifty boxes, and land them on the island of Aneityum. This would cost one hundred pounds.

After leaving Melbourne, the missionaries discovered that this captain was very different from the kindly captain of the *Clutha.* He cursed and beat his men and was an all-round tyrant. Fortunately only twelve days after leaving Melbourne the missionaries arrived near Aneityum. The captain dropped anchor about ten miles from shore.

"Can't you bring us a little nearer to our destination?" asked Paton.

"I agreed to take you to Aneityum. There it is," replied the heartless captain, pointing to the island in the distance.

After a time a trader's boat pulled alongside to see what the *Frances P. Sage* wanted. Mr. Paton hastily wrote a note to Dr. Geddie, a missionary on Aneityum, and the trader took it back to the island with him.

The next morning Dr. Geddie came on the little mission schooner, the *John Knox,* accompanied by smaller boats manned by the willing hands of Christian islanders. From the deck of the *Frances P. Sage* the missionaries' boxes were lowered onto the boats. Then the missionaries made the transfer to the *John Knox.* The ropes were cast off and the *John Knox* began to pull away from the *Frances P. Sage.* As she did so, her mainmast caught on a projection on the larger ship and was snapped in two. As the mast crashed to the deck, Paton pulled his wife to one side just in time to save her life.

Being deprived of her mainsail, the *John Knox* was helpless. The captain of the *Frances P. Sage* saw that the schooner was badly damaged, but sailed off for Penang without offering to help the mission party. The wind came up and the schooner slowly drifted farther and farther from Aneityum toward another island, in spite of the efforts of the other boats to tow it.

"What place is that?" Mrs. Paton asked Dr. Geddie.

"Unfortunately, that is the island of Tanna," he replied.

"Why? What is unfortunate about it?"

"Like most of the islands in this area, Tanna is inhabited by cannibals. Should our ship ground there, the islanders would kill and eat us and plunder our goods."

Meanwhile, another missionary, Dr. Inglis, who lived on another part of Aneityum, heard of the arrival of the new missionaries. He came in his boat and spotted the *John Knox* on the horizon. Realizing her danger, he urged his island lads to pull hard. At last, close beside the helpless *John Knox,* he threw a rope which was soon made fast. The additional help was just what was needed. There followed several hours of heavy rowing in tropical heat. Finally, just as darkness fell, the Patons stepped onto the tiny dock at

Paton pulled his wife to safety just in time as the mast
snapped and crashed to the deck.

Aneityum in the New Hebrides. It was exactly four months and fourteen days since they had sailed away from Scotland.

The Patons enjoyed visiting the missionaries and their converts and learning something of the way of life on the island. After a few weeks all the missionaries held a conference during which it was agreed the Patons would work on the island of Tanna, the cannibal island they were afraid the drifting *John Knox* would reach. Some disquieting thoughts must have occurred to John and his wife at this assignment. But John took courage as he looked at the Aneityumese who only ten years before had been cannibals, and were now followers of Jesus. What God had done through the missionaries on Aneityum, surely He could do through their labors on Tanna.

Dr. Geddie advised that Mrs. Paton remain on Aneityum while her husband and Dr. Inglis went to Tanna to purchase mission sites and erect homes for themselves. With several helpers from Aneityum the two men sailed across the sea to Tanna. There they purchased a piece of land and paid for it with axes, blankets, fishhooks, and trinkets the islanders coveted. This would eventually be Dr. Inglis' place of labor. From there they sailed around the island to Port Resolution, where another piece of land was bought from the natives to be used for the Patons' mission station.

The men then set to work, burning coral blocks for making plastering lime, and collecting sugar-cane leaf with which to thatch the house. In three weeks a simple home was completed. It was truly in a beautiful location; a hill rose sharply in the rear while the front sloped gently down to the seashore only a hundred yards away.

John was shocked at the condition of the Tannese people. The men and women wore only the scantiest covering and the children wore no clothing at all. The people were filthy and extremely excitable. John's heart almost sank as he thought of their degraded condition, and he wondered if anything could be done for them. They seemed scarcely better, and no cleaner, than the pigs that grunted around

34

every island hut. But when he thought of the Aneityum islanders who had been in the same condition, his faith and hope revived.

The islanders on Tanna were divided into a number of tribes. Some of them were known as harbor people and some as inland people. Hostilities between the tribes were common. Even while Paton was building his house, war broke out between two adjoining tribes.

It was difficult to continue working on the house while only a few hundred yards away the bush rang with the excited cries of the warriors, and muskets banged continuously like firecrackers. The fighting kept up most of the day. Once, when the warriors came very near, Dr. Inglis leaned against a post, prayed silently, then reminded his companion that the walls of Jerusalem in Nehemiah's day had been built in troublesome times, so why not the mission house on Tanna?

That evening an Aneityum teacher told them that five or six men had been killed in the fighting. The bodies had fallen into the hands of the harbor people, who ate them during the night.

The next morning their Aneityum cook said, "Missi [the local title for a missionary], this is a dark land. At the spring where I always get pure water for you, they have washed the bodies of the dead and it is full of blood. I cannot use it. What shall I do for your water?"

Dr. Inglis said they would drink coconut milk until the rains came to purify the water.

The next night the quiet was shattered by a wild wailing. In the morning John and Dr. Inglis learned that a warrior, wounded in the recent fighting, had died and his widow had been strangled so that she could accompany her husband to the spirit world.

When the house was almost finished, the two men returned to Aneityum, where the Patons prepared to proceed with their boxes to Tanna at the first opportunity. The captain of a trading schooner agreed to move the missionaries and their goods to Port Resolution for five pounds. Mr. Copeland and John and Janet Paton landed on Tanna to begin their work on the fifth of November, 1858.

The islanders crowded round, particularly the women and children. They had met white traders but most of them had never seen a white woman before. The missionaries felt especially helpless because they did not know a single word of the Tannese language. But they smiled at the islanders, and some of the islanders smiled in return as they went back to their village houses.

One day two Tannese came again to the mission house. Picking up some article that happened to be lying on the ground, one man asked, "Nungsi nari enu?"

He must be asking, What is this? thought Paton. Picking up a piece of wood, he repeated the words, "Nungsi nari enu?"

The two men smiled to hear him using their language. They gave him the word he had asked for. From then on, he continued pointing to various objects, repeating the question, and jotting down the answers. Thus his knowledge of the language increased daily.

The Patons realized that they faced constant dangers from the heathen. They knew that the islanders had perhaps welcomed them at first with the thought in mind that they would have plenty of trade goods to plunder when they decided either to kill their visitors or drive them away.

Mr. Paton had built his house on the site where two former missionaries, Nisbet and Turner, had lived for several months, vainly trying to establish a mission on Tanna. The rage of the heathen had been so great that they had fled by night in an open boat onto the ocean, leaving their goods to be plundered. Fortunately a passing whaling ship picked the two men up, or they would surely have been lost. Sixteen years later, Mr. Paton and his companion occupied the same site.

From a high point on Tanna the dim outline of Erromanga, often referred to as the Martyr Isle, could be seen.

On that island the well-known missionary, John Williams, and his companion, Harris, had landed nearly twenty years before. Within a few minutes of going ashore, the two men had been clubbed to death by the savage inhabitants. Their bodies had provided a cannibal feast.

Mr. Paton was to learn by sad experience that he had made a serious mistake in building his house down near the sea. When the rainy season began, both Mr. and Mrs. Paton suffered severely from fever. One day a local chief said to Paton, "Missi, if you stay here, you will soon die! No Tanna-man would sleep so low down as you do in this damp weather, or he would die. You must go and sleep on the hill and then you will have better health."

Paton immediately decided to move his house, but his decision came too late. On February 12, only three months after her arrival on Tanna, Mrs. Paton gave birth to a son. For two days mother and child seemed to do well, and great joy filled the father's heart. But Mrs. Paton did not regain her strength. An attack of fever followed which laid her low. Tossing on her bed, she suffered intense fever, and then chilling cold. It was an unequal struggle and could have only one end. On the fourteenth day of her illness, as the sun went down, she was heard to murmur, "O that my dear mother were here! She is a good woman, my mother, a jewel of a woman."

Seeing Mr. Copeland standing near, she spoke again. "Oh, Mr. Copeland, you must not think that I regret coming here, and leaving my mother. If I had the same thing to do over again, I would do it with far more pleasure, yes, with all my heart."

Not long after this she fell asleep. Mr. Paton thought his cup of sorrow was overflowing, but there was one more loss to come. A few days later his little son, whom he had named after his grandfather, Peter Robert Robson, also died.

Although suffering from fever himself, Paton prepared the grave in which he buried mother and child together. Having outlined it with coral blocks he sprinkled over it a quantity of finely ground white coral. He bitterly regretted the mistakes of the past six months. If only he had left Janet on Aneityum during the rainy season. If only he had built his home on the hill. It was a severe loss, not only for him, but also for the mission. Mrs. Paton had already started daily classes with a group of eight women, teaching them how to care for their homes, their husbands, and their children.

One day a canoe arrived from Aneityum and Mr. Paton was handed a letter from the workers there. Reading it, he was surprised and saddened to learn that his friend and only companion, Mr. Copeland, was requested to move to the station at Aneityum to care for the work there. Dr. Inglis would soon be going to England where he hoped to get the first New Testament in the Aneityum language printed. Sorrowfully Paton bade his companion farewell, hoping that he would be back within six or eight months.

Copeland never returned to Tanna, but was sent to the island of Ertuna. Paton was now more lonely than he had ever been in his life.

About three months after the death of Mrs. Paton, Bishop Selyn and another worker, Patterson, called at Port Resolution. Both had met Mrs. Paton on Aneityum a short time before, when she had been the very picture of health. Now the two men walked with Paton to the grave, where they stood, Paton weeping on one side, and Patterson, himself later to die a martyr on the island of Nakupu, sobbing silently on the other. The good bishop poured out his heart to God, calling down Heaven's richest blessings and comfort on Mr. Paton.

That evening as they sat in Paton's lonely home the bishop asked a question.

"John, don't you think you need a change? Come on the ship with me to Australia for a three-month rest."

Paton looked at the good bishop, then shook his head.

"I shall stay here," he said.

SURPRISED THIEVES

"MISSI, Missi, come quickly."

Mr. Paton laid aside the book he had been reading and looked into the face of one of the mission teachers.

"What's the matter, Abraham?"

"Oh, Missi, we cannot tell you. You will have to come and see for yourself." Seldom had Paton seen such excitement in one of his teachers.

The teachers led Paton out to a portion of the land he had bought for the mission. They pointed to some reeds stuck into the ground, crossing all the paths leading into the mission area. Paton was mystified by the teachers' excitement, and he could not understand why they were so afraid.

"What do these reeds mean?" he asked.

"Missi, don't you understand? Those are taboo reeds. If we continue to work this land, the Tanna men will kill us in the night."

"But we bought this land from the chiefs when we first arrived. Why should they want to take it away from us now?"

"Oh, Missi, you do not understand the Tannese people. They don't want the worship, but they covet everything you have."

Paton immediately sent for Nouka and Miaki, two of the most powerful chiefs in the area, and asked them why his land had been placed under taboo.

"The blankets you gave were sufficient for the ground where you have your house," the men explained, "but they are not enough for the rest of the land. You must pay for the land also."

A few days later, when a trading vessel dropped anchor in Port Resolution Bay, John Paton bought the goods the chiefs demanded. These he handed to them in the presence of many witnesses. Then the chief carefully removed the reeds and declared that the taboo was lifted. Actually this was the third time that piece of land had been bought. It was first paid for by the two missionaries who had been driven away sixteen years before Paton arrived. Unfortunately, this third payment gave the Tannese the idea that by threatening the missionary, they could extort from him anything they wanted.

More trouble came with a drought that severely reduced food supplies on Tanna. The teachers warned Paton that the medicine man was telling the people the rain would not come until the white man was driven from the island. Chief Nowar, who showed some interest in the gospel, visited Paton.

"Pray to your God, Missi," the chief pleaded. "If rain does not come, they will drive you from the island."

So the missionary and his teachers prayed for rain. Within forty-eight hours it began to rain. Unfortunately, it rained so much that some of the crops were spoiled. Next came a dreadful hurricane, knocking down many coconut trees and demolishing houses and gardens.

"The island gods are angry because we have allowed a worshiper of the God of heaven to come here," declared the medicine man. "You will have no peace until he is driven away."

Bands of armed men began prowling around the mission house, watching for the missionary, so that they might shoot him or club him to death. Then the storms ended, the sun came out, and for weeks everyone was busy repairing fences and replanting the gardens.

On Sundays Paton and one of his teachers visited some of the nearby villages. Few of the men would listen to the gospel story, but the women and children responded. The missionary prayed earnestly that some light might break through into their darkened hearts.

Paton was greatly troubled as he saw how the men treated their wives. Not only were the women beaten severely to make them work, but when a chief died, his wives were all killed and eaten. Once when John Paton was telling the Tanna men how wicked it was to treat their wives this way, one old chief boldly replied, "If we did not beat our women, they would never work; they would not fear and obey us; but when we have beaten and killed a few of them and have feasted on two or three, the rest are all very good for a long time."

The brother of a chief from another island, who was visiting Tanna, became sick. John was blamed for the illness. A number of chiefs met together to decide what to do.

"Since Missi came, we have had much sickness and many deaths on our island," one chief declared.

"We hate Missi because he comes here and spoils all the customs we have received from our fathers," said another.

"If we let him stay, he will spoil our women so they will no longer work for us," said a third.

For hours they continued talking. Miaki, the war chief, offered to lead a band of men at night to the white man's house and set it on fire. If the missionary tried to escape the fire, they would club him in the dark.

Suddenly, for no apparent reason, one great warrior chief leaped to his feet, swung aloft his mighty war club, and smashed it into the ground.

"The man that kills Missi must first kill me!" he shouted. "The men that kill the mission teachers must first kill me and my people—for we shall defend them till death."

Instantly another chief arose and said practically the same thing. Nothing further could be done in the face of such determination, and the whole assembly broke up in confusion, each chief heading for his own village.

Although Paton continued to hold village meetings, only a few of the men would attend. But under cover of darkness, several would sneak quietly to the missionary's house, and discuss the Christian religion.

One chief came many times. One night he remarked, "I would be an *Awfuaki* man [a Christian] were it not that all the rest of the village would laugh at me, and I could never stand that!" Sadly he went away, almost persuaded to be a Christian, but afraid of what others might say.

The Tannese, being expert thieves, were extremely clever at taking what they wanted from the missionary without being caught. If one was standing in Paton's house when some article fell to the floor, he would quickly step on it, fasten it firmly between his toes, and walk out of the house with no look of shame or embarrassment on his face. Paton lost many things which he greatly needed: a pair of scissors, knives, dishes, and, one by one, his pots and pans.

The people were not ashamed of stealing, but felt greatly shamed if caught doing so. One sunshiny morning after several rainy days, Paton and two of the teachers' wives were busy hanging Paton's bedclothes over a rope line to dry. Suddenly Miaki came running up breathlessly, and told Paton he wanted to talk to him. Miaki dashed into the house and Paton had to follow him. Suddenly the wife of one of the teachers shouted, "Missi, come quickly! Miaki's men are stealing your sheets and blankets."

Paton dashed out of the house, only to find that his bedding had disappeared. He turned to Miaki and asked, "How could you do that to me? You know that I need those clothes."

Miaki pretended to be very angry, and smashed furiously at the bushes with his club. "I will catch those fellows and make them return all of Missi's things. I will smash them with this club."

The day came when Paton did not have a single cooking pot left. He offered Miaki a blanket if the chief could get one of his kettles back to him. After a few days, Miaki brought it, but without a lid. This, he explained, was with a chief on the other side of the island. It could not possibly be returned.

"Wants another bribe for the lid," muttered Paton to himself.

One morning a few weeks later a whole group of greatly excited Tannese men came rushing toward Paton's house. They were shouting.

"Missi! Missi! There is a god or a ship on fire, or something of fear coming over the sea! We can see no flames, but it smokes like a volcano. Is it a spirit, or a god, or a ship on fire? What is it? What is it?"

Soon the house was surrounded by fifty or sixty trembling warriors. John immediately guessed that it was a steamer, possibly even a warship. He immediately excused himself, to get ready to receive visitors.

"Missi, Missi, come quick and see. Tell us what it is!" But Paton was not to be hurried.

"I cannot go now," he replied. "I must dress in my best clothes; it is most likely one of Queen Victoria's men-of-war coming to ask me if your conduct is good or bad, if you are stealing my property or threatening my life or how you are using me."

"Missi, will it be a ship of war?"

"I think it will. Now I have no time to speak to you, I must get on my best clothing."

"Missi, please listen and tell us. Will he ask you if we have been stealing your things?"

"I expect he will."

"And what will you tell him?"

"I must tell him the truth. If he asks, I will tell him no lies."

"Oh, Missi, tell him not. Everything shall be brought back to you at once, and no one will be allowed to steal from you anymore."

"Then you had better hurry. Everything must be brought

"Missi, there is something out there on the sea smoking like a volcano. Is it a god—or what?"

back before the ship arrives. Now, be gone. I must prepare to meet the great chief of the man-of-war."

Away they rushed in all directions. Up to this time it had been impossible to find anyone willing to admit having taken anything. But now the people ran back, carrying spoons, kettles, blankets, knives, and many other household articles.

"Missi, what shall we do with these things? Please come and look at them."

"Just make a pile there by the door. I have no time to speak with you."

"Missi, Missi, please come and look. Tell us if all the stolen property has been returned."

Paton stepped outside the door and hastily glanced over the large pile of goods. He did not have time to examine it carefully, but he did notice that the lid of the pot he had gotten back was still missing.

"I do not see the lid of my kettle."

"No, Missi, it is still on the other side of the island. Please tell him not, for we have sent a swift messenger who will return with it tomorrow."

Seeing some of the chiefs of the harbor area present, Paton called the chiefs Nauka, Miaki, and Nowar to him.

"When the commander of the great warship comes ashore, you must not run away in fright, for then he will want to know why you flee. If he does, then I must tell him."

Miaki replied, "We are in black fear, but we will keep near you, and our bad conduct to you is finished from now on."

The warship sailed into the harbor, the anchor was dropped, and a rowboat lowered. Sailors rowed the captain and some of his officers to the landing, where Paton and the chiefs awaited him. Captain Vernon had heard of the dangers to which the missionary had been exposed on Tanna, and had decided to investigate.

All eyes were fastened on the handsome commander and his men, well armed, and dressed in splendid uniforms.

These uniforms put an idea into Miaki's head. Leaving the line he dashed to his hut and donned a soldier's red coat he had gotten someplace, which he buttoned around the top of his otherwise naked body. Then with great pride he rushed back and pushed his way to a place next to the missionary. The English captain looked at him.

"What sort of character is this?" he asked John.

"This is Miaki, our great war chief," replied Paton quite loudly, and then added under his breath, "Be careful what you say. He knows a little English and might understand you."

"The contemptible creature," muttered the captain, but Miaki only grinned, not understanding.

When Captain Vernon returned to his ship, he invited the chiefs to visit the deck of the man-of-war. They were astonished at what they saw.

Then the captain had two cannon fired out to sea. The chiefs were terrified as they saw the shells splash into the ocean. But then a shell was discharged toward the island. It crashed into a large coconut grove, cutting down coconut trees as though they were straw. At this the chiefs were filled with terror and begged to be put ashore. What wonderful stories they doubtless had to tell the villagers for days to come!

Paton now decided that he should build a new house on the hill behind his first dwelling, away from the malarial lowlands around the bay. Already he had suffered fourteen attacks of malaria. But just at the time he started to build he was hit by the worst attack to that time. When the attack came, he tried to climb to the top of the hill where he could breathe wholesome air. But he was so weak that when he had climbed two thirds of the way, he became faint and felt that he was dying.

His faithful Aneityumese servant, Abraham, and his wife carried Paton to the shade of a tree and laid him on coconut leaves.

Night and day for how long John did not know, the

teacher and his wife cared for their beloved Missi. Had they not done so he would have died. To Paton it was a wonderful thing. In the days of his youth, Abraham had been a cannibal. If the love of God could do that for one man, might it not do the same for the people of Tanna?

When he was well, Paton built his house and moved into it. From there he continued visiting the villages, preaching the gospel of Jesus to all who would listen.

DANGER

PATON had many problems with the heathen Tannese, who were treacherous and thievish. But more of a problem to him were the white men who came as traders. Most of them were wicked men who contaminated the natives and cheated them at every opportunity.

One such man, a Captain Winchester, lived on the island at the head of the bay where John had his station. He was a trader who made his living by bartering with the natives, and selling to passing ships the pigs and chickens he took in. One of his items of trade was muskets and ammunition.

A time of comparative peace settled down on the island, caused partly as a result of John's influence and partly because of the visit of the warship, which had made the Tannese fearful of bringing down on them the wrath of the "great Chief" of the ship.

This state of things did not please Captain Winchester a bit, for it cut down on his business considerably.

He began to show a great interest in the affairs of the island, and gave all the chiefs in the area powder, caps, and balls. He loaned muskets to some of them.

"Don't be afraid of fighting," he told them. "I will let you have all the ammunition you want."

John protested the traders' actions, but the captain was unmoved. "Peace is not for me," he stated. "I prefer war."

Urged on by the captain, the local tribes began to fight against neighboring tribes without any cause.

As soon as the war began, the trader wickedly increased the price of ammunition constantly until it took a large hog to pay for a few ounces of powder. Into his yard came pigs and chickens on which the captain made a good profit.

A younger brother of Miaki, the war chief, named Rarip, had taken a great interest in the teachings of the missionary. When war began he went to live with Paton in the mission house.

"Missi, I hate all this fighting," he said. "It is not good to kill men. I will live with you?"

Paton made him welcome, and he lived with him for several days. But after the war had gone on for some time Miaki forced him to join the fighting men. However, at the first opportunity, Rarip escaped into the bush and returned to Paton.

Enraged, Miaki once more forced Rarip to join the fighting. This time he made him stay right beside him so he could keep an eye on his 18-year-old brother.

As Miaki's warriors rushed against their enemies during the next battle, a bullet pierced Rarip's breast, and he fell dead in his brother's arms. Rarip's body was carried back to the village, and John was called. He found the people wailing, cutting themselves with pieces of bamboo, and knocking their heads against trees. Paton took Rarip, wrapped him in a piece of cloth, and gave him a Christian burial.

The war continued and many others were killed. The warriors began to realize that the cause of all the trouble was Captain Winchester.

"You led us into this war," Miaki accused him. "You deceived us. Now Rarip is dead and many others. Your life shall go for his."

Captain Winchester now showed that he was a coward. Trembling, he begged Paton to let him and his wife sleep at the mission house. But John would not agree. For him to permit this would be to associate himself with the captain's crimes.

The captain became so terrified that he slept in his boat each night, anchored in the middle of the bay, his rifle beside him, ready to flee if attacked. By day he kept watch on the shore, poised to fly. Finally, a trading vessel came by and he left, to the gratification of all.

The war continued for another three months, after which Paton managed to bring it to an end.

Slowly, but with much determined resistance, the influence of the gospel grew. One who did much to spread the gospel was an Aneityumese teacher, Namuri. With his wife he was living in the village nearest to Paton's house. By his pure and humble life, and by his teaching, Namuri did much by his good example.

One morning a "sacred man," or witch doctor, who hated the message Namuri was bringing, threw a *kawas,* or killing stone, at the teacher. Namuri managed to avoid the stone, but it caught his hand and cut it deeply. The priest then sprang at him and beat at him savagely with his heavy club. Namuri managed to escape and staggered to the mission house.

"Oh, Missi, Missi," he gasped. "Quick, escape for your life. They are coming to kill you for they hate Jehovah and the worship!"

Paton hurried to where the bleeding man lay on the ground, and bathed and bandaged his wounds. All the time the angry priest and his followers stood at a distance, not daring to come closer. John kept Namuri at the mission house for three or four weeks, until he had recovered. By that time some of the villagers had invited him to return to the village. But Paton insisted that this could not be until the man who had tried to kill Namuri be punished.

The chiefs then tied up the sacred man and invited Paton to come and see him punished. After a long talk, the sacred man promised never to molest the teacher again.

Paton now urged Namuri not to return to the village for a while. The teacher shook his head.

"Missi, I must go back," he said. "I know they are bad

people, and they want to kill me. But I remember when I was a heathen and the missionary came to my island. I joined with others in trying to kill him. Suppose he had become frightened and gone away? I would still be a heathen. Do you not see that I must go back?"

Reluctantly Paton agreed, but before long his worst fears were realized. One morning while Namuri was kneeling in prayer, that same priest sprang upon him, clubbed him severely, and finally left him for dead. It took the poor teacher several hours to crawl to the mission house. Paton did all he could for the man, but his injuries were too great. The next morning, brave Namuri breathed a prayer that brought tears to Paton's eyes.

"O Lord Jesus," he whispered, "forgive them. Oh, take not away all Thy servants from Tanna! Take not Thy worship from this dark island! O God, bring all the Tannese to love and follow Jesus."

And then, having prayed, Namuri died.

Paton had spent many months reducing the Tannese language to writing. Although he had never studied printing, he determined to publish a portion of the gospel of Matthew in Tannese. Thomas Binnie, a Glasgow friend, sent him a small printing press and some type. Hour after hour the missionary practiced setting type. Finally he felt that he was ready to print the first edition of his Testament. But it took him quite a while to discover how to arrange the pages so they would fold into the proper sections of the book. Finally one morning at one o'clock, he ran off the first sheet. He held it up, folded it, and found that it was right at last.

That was one of the most joyful moments of his life. In a book published many years later, he described how he danced around the press, threw his hat into the air and shouted for joy until he began to wonder whether he had lost his senses. He wrote of how this experience made him think of David who danced before the ark of God when escorting it to Jerusalem.

Not long after this, two ships visited Tanna. The first was

At two in the morning Paton finally got the press working.
He threw his hat in the air from delight.

an American boat, the *Camden Packet*, which had been away from New England for three years catching whales in the South Seas. The captain, a sincere Christian, invited Paton on board to preach to him and his crew. It was a bit difficult, for Paton had not preached in English for several years. Captain Allen offered to take Paton to a place of safety, but that brave man refused to forsake his mission. The sailors repaired a large hole in Paton's boat, patching it neatly and charging him nothing.

The second vessel was of an entirely different type. It belonged to a Frenchman, and was fitted out and armed like a man-of-war. The crew were nearly all slaves, ruled with an iron hand. But this captain was also kind to Paton, offering to take him anywhere he might choose to go. Paton refused to leave his work.

During his years on Tanna, Paton never felt completely free from danger. One day as he was working in his garden, he became aware that an islander was standing nearby with a gun pointed directly at him. He lifted his heart to God, then calmly went about his work. Knowing that only a miracle could save him, he calmly awaited whatever would happen. For three hours the man continued to prowl around with his gun. Apparently he was unable to pull the trigger, and at last left in disgust.

Another day a war chief with a large body of armed men surrounded the place where Paton was working. At a word from their leader, each man raised his musket and aimed it at the white man. Every second Paton expected to hear the roar that would end his life. Each man seemed to be urging his neighbor to pull the trigger, but no one did. After enduring an anxious hour of this, Paton was relieved to see the warriors withdraw into the bush.

The people of Tanna were very superstitious. They believed that evil spirits could cause all kinds of misfortune. They once told Paton that he was responsible for all the troubles on their island, because he worshiped a new God never before known on Tanna. If he would only go away they would have no more death, sickness, hurricanes, or drought. Paton suggested that all these things happened because they did not worship the true God. This was a new thought, and the savages withdrew to discuss the problem.

A few days later, they returned with their answer.

"We do not blame you, and you must not blame us for causing these troubles and deaths." Paton quite willingly agreed with their suggestion.

One of the most dreaded Tannese customs was that of killing an enemy by means of sorcery called *nahak*. The idea was that if an enemy could obtain any scrap left over from food a person had eaten, he could have a sacred man, a witch doctor, cast a spell over that person and cause his death. Once, when talking to the people of a certain village about the power of God, some sacred men challenged him. If only they could get hold of some food he had tasted, they would show their *nahak* was more powerful than Missi's God.

Paton determined to strike one telling blow at the superstition. Seeing a woman standing nearby with a bunch of plumlike native fruit in her hand, he asked if she would give him some.

"Take all you wish," she replied, holding them out to him. He took three of them.

"Now look at me," said Paton. He calmly took a bite from each, then handed them to the sacred men sitting nearby.

"These men say they can kill me by *nahak*. I say they cannot. In the presence of all of you, I give them this fruit from which I have eaten."

The sacred men took the fruit and got ready to perform their ritual. The Tannese fled in fear; they were terrified that they might be touched by the curse.

The sacred men went to one of their sacred trees and began their incantations, looking wildly at Paton every now and then, expecting him to fall dead.

Eager to have them see that their superstition could not work when God was protecting him, Paton urged, "Be quick!

Stir up your gods to help you! I am not killed yet, I am perfectly well."

Finally one of the sacred men said, "We cannot kill Missi today. But we will gather all the sacred men on the island and Missi will be dead before his next day of rest comes."

"Very well," Paton replied. "I challenge all your priests to kill me by *nahak*. If I come back here next Sunday and stand before you in perfect health, then you must all admit that your gods have no power over me, and that the true and living Jehovah God protects me."

Through the rest of the week the conch shells sounded, summoning sacred men from all over the island. But their efforts were in vain. The following Sunday the missionary strode into the village. Villagers from miles around were present.

"My love to you, my friends," Paton began. "I have come again to talk to you about the Jehovah God and His worship." Someone asked the sacred men why they could not kill Missi.

"It is true we have not killed Missi," they said. "But we are sure that Missi is a sacred man himself. Also he is protected by his God, who unfortunately for us, is stronger than the gods of Tanna."

That is just what Paton had hoped they would say.

"Yes, truly," he replied. "My Jehovah God is stronger than your gods. He protected me and helped me; for He is the only living and true God, the only God that can hear and answer prayer. Your gods cannot hear prayer. If you will give your hearts to Him, He will hear and answer you and protect you from danger. Now come close to me, and I will tell you more about my Jehovah God."

The people gathered around him. Suddenly a sacred man approached, shaking a long spear.

Paton spoke to him calmly.

"Yes, you can kill me with a spear; but you promised to do it by *nahak!*"

The man did not dare to throw his spear, for the people

were standing so close to the missionary that there was danger he might hit one of them. But he brooded over the shame of his disgrace. For many days after that, as Paton went about his work, this man followed him, the great spear always in his hand. However, angels of God prevented him from throwing it, for the work of John Paton was not yet finished on Tanna.

RAGE OF THE WICKED

PATON was happy when two missionaries from Canada, a Mr. and Mrs. Johnson, came to Tanna to help him. Together the two men built a second house. Mr. and Mrs. Johnson spent many hours each day learning the Tannese language with Mr. Paton as their teacher. Paton was hopeful that soon the Tannese would show more interest in the gospel story. Perhaps, thought the missionaries, a new day is dawning for Tanna. But these fond hopes were soon blasted.

One day three or four trading ships anchored in the harbor of Port Resolution. Rowboats came ashore, and trading with the islanders began. The captains called on Mr. Paton.

"We know how to bring down our proud Tannese!" one of them boasted. "We'll humble them!"

"What do you mean? Surely you don't plan to attack these poor people."

"No, we've got something better than bullets for killing them. We've sent measles among them, and that will wipe them out by the score! It will sweep them all away so white men can occupy their soil."

The missionary was filled with horror; but he soon found that the captain had indeed told the truth. Four young Tanna men had been enticed on board one of the ships. They were seized and thrust into the hold, where they spent the night with other islanders who were lying ill with measles. In the morning the captain put the four men back on the island. From these the disease spread all over Tanna. In a short time the disease spread and became a plague against which the islanders had little resistance.

The friendly feelings of the Tannese toward the missionaries turned now to hatred. White men had brought death to their island; therefore the white men must die.

If ever there had been a time when Paton needed his helpers, it was now, and at this very time he lost them. Thirteen Aneityumese teachers died of measles. And when the mission ship, *John Knox*, stopped at Tanna all the surviving teachers and their wives prepared to leave on it. Paton discovered that even faithful Abraham was packing his things. He asked sadly, "Abraham, are you also going to leave me here on Tanna to fight the Lord's battles alone?"

"Missi, will you remain?"

"Yes, Abraham, but the danger to your life is now so great that I dare not plead with you to stay, for we may both be killed. However, I cannot leave the Lord's work now."

The teacher gazed at his boxes and bundles for a few moments, then he looked at the missionary.

"Missi," he said, "our danger is very great."

"Yes, and I once thought you would not leave me to face it alone."

"Missi, would you like me to remain with you, seeing my wife is lying in her grave here?"

"Yes, I would like you to remain, but only if it is your own free choice."

"Then Missi, I am going to stay with you as long as you live on Tanna."

And he kept his word throughout the storm of troubles that soon broke on the island.

A few evenings later two fiercely painted warriors carrying war clubs arrived at Paton's house. They said they needed medicine for a sick boy. Paton led them to a back room where he stored his medicines. Suddenly it flashed into his mind that the men had come to murder the missionaries. Paton handed them the medicine and asked them to go, but they stood where they were, defiantly facing him. He began to walk toward them, ordering them to go.

The men turned to leave. Mr. Johnson, who had been in the house, had left just before them. As the warriors left the house Johnson was just stooping to pick up a kitten. One warrior lifted his huge club and aimed it at Mr. Johnson's back. Glancing up, Mr. Johnson saw the club and fell screaming to the ground. The other warrior then sprang forward with raised club. But at that moment Paton's two dogs sprang at them. Hindered in their plans, the men fled.

Mr. Johnson was never the same after that fearful evening, and from then on he had great difficulty sleeping. But one day Mrs. Johnson came to Paton, crying, "My husband is sleeping so soundly that I cannot wake him."

John was at the worst stage of a malarial attack, but he hastened to Mr. Johnson's bedside to discover that he was suffering from tetanus—his jaw was firmly locked. They managed to arouse him from his coma, but in a few days he died. After he was buried, Mrs. Johnson went to Aneityum, where she taught in the school and eventually married another missionary.

One of the men who worked with Paton was Kowia, a chief of the highest rank. As a youth he had gone to the island of Aneityum, become a Christian, and had married a Christian wife. He had returned to Tanna to help Paton.

When he returned to his home island his people tried to get him to give up his faith. If he did not, they said, they would not recognize him as their chief. Boldly he had answered, "Take it all. I shall still stand by Missi and the worship of Jehovah."

The Tannese did everything they could to make life miserable for Kowia. Once when he was at the mission house some villagers came with fowls to sell. Kowia paid for them. But then one man shamelessly tried to sell them again to the missionary.

"Don't buy them, Missi," Kowia said. "I have already bought them for you."

At this the man who had tried to cheat began to mock the chief. Kowia's eyes flashed. Looking around him he exclaimed, "Missi, they think that because I am now a Christian I have become a coward. But I will show them for once that I am still their chief and have not lost my courage."

He sprang at the nearest man and wrenched the heavy war club from his hands. Swinging it over his head like a toy, he cried, "Come, any of you, come all of you, against your chief! My Jehovah God makes my heart and arms strong. Christians are men of peace, but they are no cowards."

The people fled before him.

Calamities continued to trouble the island. A violent hurricane struck, knocking down trees and tearing up gardens from one end of the island to the other. The church was leveled to the ground, and only one room remained of Mr. Paton's house to protect him from the fury of the storm. Again it was declared that all such disasters were caused by the presence of the missionary. Armed men prowled around the house continually, and Paton did not know at what moment his life might be taken.

One day chief Nowar came to see Mr. Paton. He was friendly to the gospel, but was not entirely dependable. "Missi, you must leave Tanna for a while or you will surely be killed."

"Nowar," Paton replied, "you know that I cannot leave this island. Do you want the light to go out on Tanna?"

"Just leave for a little time, Missi, until the danger is gone. Miaki is telling the people that he is going to kill you himself."

But Paton insisted that he could not leave.

Nowar pretended to be very angry because his advice was not taken. Fearful for his life because he was known to be a friend of the missionary, he took off his clothes and painted his body to prove that he was still a heathen.

One night Paton heard his goats bleating in their pen

60

behind his house. He seized a lantern and hurried out to see what was wrong. At the goat house he was suddenly surrounded by a band of armed men. This might be his last hour, and he knew it. He began to talk kindly but firmly to the savages, pointing out that he had come to the island only to help them. Although he was not afraid to die, he said, he would much rather live and guide them to ways of happiness. One by one his enemies slipped away in the darkness, and presently Paton found himself alone. God had delivered him again!

About that time a cruel deed done on the nearby island of Erromanga emboldened the hearts of the heathen on Tanna. Mr. and Mrs. Gordon, missionaries who had worked on Erromanga for about four years, were murdered. A few days after the news of this tragedy reached Tanna, the Tannese marched around Paton's house shouting, "Our love to the men of Erromanga. They are better than we are. We talk about killing our Missi, they go ahead and do it. Our love to the Erromangans."

One evening a group of natives gathered near the missionary's house. Abraham went out to learn what they wanted.

"Teacher," they urged, "if you want to save your life return to your own island."

Abraham answered, "I will never leave Missi."

That evening as Abraham and Paton had worship together Abraham prayed a prayer in which he pleaded for protection but left all to God's will, and thanked his heavenly Father for Jesus. Paton wrote later: "His great simple soul poured itself out to God; and my heart melted within me as it had never done under any prayer poured from the lips of cultured Christian men!"

So continuous was the danger now that Paton seldom removed his clothes when he slept at night. His faithful dog was always on the alert. No sound escaped her attention, and with a sharp bark she would waken Paton immediately. On one occasion she pulled the blanket off the sleeping

Sensing danger, the dog pulled the blanket off the sleeping
Paton to get his attention.

man to catch his attention. In a marvelous way God caused the heathen to fear that small dog, although one blow with a club would have ended her life.

In this time of trial poor Nowar continued to waver. He seemed to want to be a Christian, but he feared the scorn of his fellow islanders. Miaki, the war chief, was full of loud boasts. Nowar repeated to Paton everything he said.

One day he reported, "Miaki says he will make a great wind and sink any man-of-war that comes here. Then he and his people will kill all the people on board. If you do not leave on the next ship the Tannese will surely kill you and Abraham. Traders will not come to sell us guns and powder while you are on the island. And we must have these things."

While they were talking together some excited natives rushed up to the mission house, shouting, "Missi, the *John Knox* is coming into the harbor, and two great ships of fire, men-of-war, are behind it, coming very fast."

Paton looked at Nowar, a suppressed smile on his face.

"Now is your chance, Nowar. Make all possible haste. Go tell Miaki to raise his great wind and sink those ships. Get all your men ready. I will tell the captain of the man-of-war that you are ready to fight him. He will be ready for battle."

But Miaki and his men did not wait to accept the challenge. They disappeared into the bush. Nowar said to Paton, "Missi, I know that my talk is all lies, but if I speak the truth they will kill me."

"Trust in Jehovah, Nowar; the God who sent these vessels to protect me will protect you, too," Paton said earnestly.

The captain of the man-of-war came on shore with Dr. John Geddie. They gathered all of the chiefs together, including Miaki. Then the captain warned the Tannese against hurting the missionary. No one need attend the worship unless he wanted to, the captain said, but they must not harm the missionary in any way. Every chief, Miaki included, solemnly promised not to threaten or hurt Paton again.

Alas, all of the promises were withdrawn as soon as the man-of-war sailed away. War broke out, and Miaki summoned all the chiefs on his side of the island. Some were in favor of standing by Missi while others wanted him driven away.

Ian, an inland chief, rose to his feet.

"You talk about driving Missi from his house and land. Whose land is it, anyway? It belonged to my people and we gave it to Missi. You have forced him to buy it from you when it was not even yours to sell."

Finally Miaki spoke. "If you want to keep Missi, take him to your own land; we will not let him live at the harbor area any longer."

At that the meeting broke up in disorder.

A few days later Chief Ian called for Paton to go with him to a meeting.

"Ian, you are not taking me away to kill me?" the missionary asked.

"Follow me quickly," was all Ian would say.

Soon they came to a large compound where a large group was assembled. Scores of Ian's men stood with muskets in their hands. Miaki, Nouka, and their followers were there looking very frightened.

"There are your enemies and ours," said Ian, pointing to Miaki and his group. "Now speak the word, and my people will sweep them all away for you. We will not shoot them unless you consent."

What an opportunity to be rid of those troublemakers! But Paton knew this was not Christ's method. He would not allow blood to be shed on his behalf. He said to Ian, "I love all of you alike. I am here to teach you to live in peace."

Ian interrupted. "Then, Missi, you will be murdered, and the worship will be destroyed."

Miaki and Nouka suddenly became courageous. "Missi's word is good. Let us all live in peace," they said. With that the gathering broke up, and Paton returned to his house.

A few weeks later Miaki vowed to kill Ian by *nahak*.

Shortly afterward Ian became sick and died with every symptom of being poisoned. Miaki now felt that the time had come to kill the missionary and plunder his goods.

Meanwhile, Ian's people decided they must avenge their chief's death, so they declared war on Miaki and his followers.

One morning Paton looked across the valley toward Miaki's village and saw a large band of armed men rushing toward the mission house. He had not a moment to lose. With Abraham and his wife, Paton slipped into the thick bush and ran rapidly to Nowar's village, leaving everything he owned on earth except two blankets, his Bible, and some Tannese translations of the Scriptures, which he carried with him.

When the three of them reached Nowar's village they found the people terrified, crying and rushing around. They were sure they would be killed by the large band of Miaki's armed men who were coming toward the village. The shore was covered with armed men rushing upon them.

"It's no use, Missi," the villagers cried. "We will all be killed and eaten today. Look at the multitude that are coming."

Chief Nowar could not flee, because in the recent fighting he had been wounded in the knee by a spear and was very lame. The missionary walked over to where Nowar was sitting on an upturned canoe. Nowar spoke.

"Missi, sit down beside me and pray to our Jehovah God, for if He does not send deliverance we are all dead men. Pray, and I will watch."

John Paton prayed as only one can pray who stands on the brink of death. The savages came to a point about three hundred yards away. Then they all stopped. Nowar touched the missionary on the knee.

"Missi, Jehovah is hearing!" he exclaimed. "They are all standing still."

Paton opened his eyes. It was indeed true. That host of warriors stood still in absolute silence for a few minutes, then they turned and marched back slowly to the other end of the harbor. Nowar and his people were in ecstasy. "Jehovah has heard Missi's prayer," they cried. "Jehovah has protected us and turned them back."

The next night Abraham crept back to the mission house to see if he could save some valuables and get some clothing. At the front door he was suddenly surrounded by a band of men.

"Stop!" said one of the leaders. "Don't kill him. Let us wait for Missi. He is sure to come for his things, and we will kill him then." Abraham was not molested.

Nowar was afraid that Miaki and his men would attack his village if they knew Paton was still there.

"You cannot remain longer in my house," he said to Paton. "My son will guide you to a large tree at the corner of my plantation. Climb to the top and remain there till the moon rises."

Paton did as the chief requested. He climbed up to a place where the branches were thick. About midnight Nowar sent his son to bring Paton back to the village.

"Missi," Nowar said, "you will have to take the boat and flee around the island to Missi Mathieson's station."

Faimungo, a friendly inland chief, spoke up.

"Missi, they are all deceiving you! The sea is so rough you cannot go on it, and Miaki has men posted to shoot you as you pass the Black Rocks. All the inland paths are guarded by armed men. I tell you the truth, for I have heard all their talk. Miaki and Karewick say they hate the worship and will kill you. They killed your goats and stole your property yesterday. Farewell!"

Paton stood praying, wondering what to do. Death seemed to await them whichever way they turned.

ESCAPE

"OUR only hope is in the canoe," Paton said. "Let us go!"

Swiftly the canoe was pushed into the water. Paton, Abraham, his wife, and two natives quickly climbed aboard. Sheltered by the land, they made good progress for about a mile. But now, on the open sea, they met the full force of the wind and waves. Water crashed over the side of their little canoe, threatening to swamp it.

"Missi, we are all drowned now," Abraham cried in an agitated voice. "We are food for the sharks. We might as well be eaten by the Tannese as by the fish. But God will give us life with Jesus in heaven."

"Let us turn the canoe around," replied the missionary. "We cannot live on such an ocean. Matthew, bail for your life!"

Slowly the canoe was reversed and the return journey begun. With the wind and waves against them, it was four hours before they finally reached shore, drenched, and dropped the paddles from their blistered hands. Exhausted, they fell on the sand and slept for a time.

When they awakened they surveyed their situation. It seemed completely hopeless. Soon Miaki learned that the mission party had returned, and he readied his men to kill Paton and his party. As Paton sat on the upturned canoe, wondering what to do, Chief Faimungo came out of the bush.

"Missi, I am sorry to see that you had to return. I am going home now. Farewell. I cannot bear to remain and see you killed today."

A sudden thought came to Mr. Paton, and with it a gleam of hope.

"Faimungo, will you let us follow you? If you will show us the path, I promise that when the next mission ship arrives I will give you three good axes, blankets, knives, and many things you desire."

Paton knew that the recent hurricanes had obliterated the paths and that only a native could guide them on the paths they needed to take to get to Mathieson's mission on the other side of the island.

"Missi, you will be killed," the chief replied. "Miaki and his men will shoot you. I dare not let you follow me. I have only about twenty men, and your presence might endanger us all."

After much urging Faimungo agreed to do nothing to stop them if they followed him. But he could promise no protection, nor could he slacken his pace should they become tired and lag behind. Faimungo and his men started out, with Paton and his little party following. All went well until about four miles from the harbor when they met a large party of Miaki's men. Every gun was raised and leveled at the missionary.

Faimungo raised his spear and said, "No, you shall not kill Missi today."

Having soothed his conscience, he strode off through the bush, and Abraham, his wife, and the others followed, leaving the missionary to face Miaki's men alone. Paton appealed to the leader.

"Sirawia, I love you all. You know I have been trying to do you good. When you and your people were sick and dying with measles I gave you the very clothing you now wear. Am I not your friend? How many times have you eaten with me at my house?"

Sirawia turned and whispered something to his follow-

68

ers. The men continued to point their guns at Paton, but he could tell that their attitude had changed. He moved gradually backward. Keeping his eyes fixed on the warriors until the bushes hid them from his view, he turned and ran as fast as he could. He soon caught up with Faimungo and the others. On and on they went, meeting other hostile groups eager to take the missionary's life but each time restrained by God's holy angels.

As they neared the center of the island Faimungo became more decided in Paton's defense. "Missi," he said, "I am not afraid now. I am feeling stronger near my own land."

But danger was by no means past. Suddenly, while resting under a tree in the open dancing ground of a village near Faimungo's territory, they heard the tramp of many men coming rapidly in their direction. Over the mountain hurried a host of shouting warriors, probably sent by Miaki to intercept and kill Paton and his company. Faimungo became very afraid again.

"Missi," he said, "go on in that path, you and your company; I will follow when I have had a smoke and a talk with these men."

Paton realized that to follow such a course would bring sure death.

"No, I will stand by your side," he replied. "If I am killed, it will be by your side. I will not leave you now."

Miaki's men surrounded Paton and his teachers. Each urged the other to shoot, but no one was willing to fire the first shot. A warrior hurled a killing stone, which grazed Abraham's cheek. A club was raised to follow the stone, but God baffled the aim of the killer. Though Paton was not without fear he knew for a certainty that God would spare his life until his work on earth was done.

Faimungo started on his way once more. Paton and his company kept close to the chief. The enemy warriors ran beside them on each side of the path with their weapons ready.

Finally they came to a stream. Faimungo, Paton, and the others started across. Their enemies did not follow, but stood watching them go. The missionary had the solemn feeling that the same hand that protected Daniel from the lions was protecting him.

Before long they met still another war party. Their leader yelled out, "Miaki and Karewick say that Missi made all the sickness and hurricanes, and we ought to kill him."

Faimungo glared at the men. "They lie about Missi. It is our own bad conduct that makes them sick."

"Well," the man replied, "even if we don't know who makes sickness, our fathers have taught us to kill all foreign men."

Faimungo clutched a club in one hand and a spear in the other, and exclaimed, "You won't kill Missi today."

"Missi," Faimungo said, "I have fulfilled my promise. I am tired and afraid. I dare not go farther. My love to you all. Now go on quickly. Three of my men will escort you to the end of my territory. Go quickly! Farewell!"

Before long the guides stopped and said, "Missi, we dare not go farther with you. Faimungo is at war with the people of the next land. Keep straight along in this path." Then they turned and went back in the direction of their own village.

Later that day the weary group passed through the land of a tribe who many years before had fought a war in which the Aneityumese were involved. Abraham feared that he might be recognized as an Aneityumese, and attacked. But, fortunately, the men were away on a war expedition. At one village a man gave them a coconut to drink and eat. How welcome this food was to the travelers, who had eaten nothing that day.

As they neared Mathieson's mission station, Mr. Mathieson, who had heard of their coming, ran to meet them.

The Mathiesons were also having problems. Their only child had just been buried, and they were almost out of food. The nearby tribes were almost as eager to kill them and plunder their goods as Miaki and his warriors around Port Resolution had been to kill Paton.

Friendly chiefs had sent word to the missionaries that

grave danger threatened them. Miaki had formed a great union of most of the Tannese chiefs. They had agreed that the time was ripe to kill every Christian on the island and return to the customs of their fathers.

In spite of threats, Mr. Paton and Mr. Mathieson continued their mission work. Sunday services were held in the church, and sometimes as many as one hundred and sixteen Tannese attended. On weekdays they visited and preached in nearby villages. The seed scattered during that troublesome time eventually bore fruit. Twenty years later a Christian church stood in that very area, with scores of members singing praise to Jesus.

One morning a group of Miaki's men came and compelled Mrs. Mathieson to show them through her home. It just happened that Mr. Paton, not wishing to be disturbed, had locked himself in a small closet to study. The warriors looked all through the house, but did not look in the closet. They left very disappointed at not being able to kill the white man.

About ten o'clock that same night Paton was awakened by the dog pulling at the blankets on his bed. Glancing out the window he saw that the house was surrounded by men. In haste he awoke the Mathiesons. In a few moments the three of them saw a glare illuminating the night. Men with flaming torches were passing to and fro, setting the thatched roof of the church on fire, as well as the reed fence connecting the church with the mission house.

They knew that in a few moments the flames would follow along the fence and set fire to the house. Then its occupants would have to choose whether to remain inside and be burned to death or to flee outside and die under the clubs of their enemies.

"That fence must be cut away from the house," Paton exclaimed. "I'll go out and do it."

"No! No!" protested Mathieson. "Let us die together. You will never return."

"Leave that with God. Quick, there is no time to waste.

"Kill him! Kill him!" shouted the savages as the flames crept nearer and nearer to Paton's house.

In a few minutes the house will be in flames. Then nothing will save us."

Paton picked up a small hatchet and went outside. The door was immediately locked from the inside. He chopped the fence from top to bottom, tearing up several feet of it and hurling it into the flames farthest away from the house.

Suddenly he was surrounded by seven or eight savages, each with a club upraised to strike him.

"Kill him! Kill him!" they shouted.

"Dare to strike me, and my Jehovah God will punish you!" Paton answered. "He protects me and will not overlook your sin in burning His church. God is on our side, a mighty helper!"

The Tannese yelled in rage. Each urged the other to strike the missionary down, but none seemed able to strike. At that very moment, when death seemed imminent, a rushing, roaring noise, like the sound of a mighty engine, was heard approaching from the south. There was no need to explain to anyone what the noise meant. A violent hurricane of wind and rain, common in the South Seas, was approaching.

In a matter of minutes the sky opened and the downpour began. The flames on the church roof hissed and went out. The wind carried the flames away from the house. The missionary stood in dense darkness. The heathen, struck with awe, lowered their clubs and spears and began to retreat, exclaiming as they went, "This is Jehovah's rain. Truly their Jehovah God is fighting for them and helping them. Away! Away! We must away."

In a few moments they had all fled into the bush. Paton returned to the mission house.

"Open and let me in," he called. "I am all alone now!" The door opened, and Paton stepped inside.

In amazement Mr. Mathieson exclaimed, "If ever, in time of need, God sent help and protection to His servants in answer to prayer, He has done so tonight. Blessed be His holy name."

During the rest of that night Paton lay awake much of the

time wondering whether the assassins would return. On the floor by his cot lay his little dog, alert and ready to warn them again should danger approach.

Soon after sunrise, some of the friends of the missionaries came and stood in the yard, weeping.

"Oh, Missi, we now see you for the last time. Your enemies who tried to destroy you last night are determined to kill you this morning and plunder your goods. This decision has made them very happy."

Helpless, the missionaries watched as an army of shouting savages, armed with spears and clubs, advanced across the little valley toward the mission house. Closer and closer they drew when suddenly another cry rose above the shouting, "Sail-O!"

Never had the missionaries heard a sweeter sound. The shouts of the heathen died away as they slunk into the bush.

For a few moments it seemed almost too good to be true. Could this be a plot on the part of their attackers to get them out into the open where they could be killed more easily? But they had to know, so they looked. Sure enough, a ship was sailing into view. Quickly Paton set fire to a pile of reeds and hung out a black shawl and a white sheet to attract attention. The ship sailed closer and hove to.

Soon two boats were lowered and rowed ashore. The missionaries rushed down to the landing, where they greeted Captain Hastings. A few days earlier his ship, the *Blue Bell*, had called at Port Resolution, where the captain had purchased from the natives there the very clothing and goods stolen from Paton's house. Calling at Aneityum next, he had met Dr. Geddie, who begged him to hasten to Tanna to rescue Mr. Paton and the Mathiesons if they were still alive. Now, in their hour of greatest danger, he had arrived.

The sailors carried the Mathiesons' goods down to the harbor. By two o'clock everything had been moved, and it was time for the missionaries to leave.

But in that strange, sad hour, Mr. Mathieson made a rash and mysterious decision. Having locked himself in his study, he informed Paton through the closed door that he had decided to remain and die on Tanna.

Of course, Paton would not listen to such a suggestion. He and Mrs. Mathieson talked through that shut door for more than three hours, but without success. Finally Paton spoke:

"It is now getting dark. Your wife must go with the vessel, but I cannot leave you alone. I shall send a note explaining why I am forced to remain, for it is certain that we shall be murdered the moment the vessel sails. I tell you that God will charge you with the guilt of our murder."

These serious words caused Mr. Mathieson to unlock the door and come out. He accompanied his wife and Paton to the landing where two boats were waiting, one loaded with their goods. They rowed out in the dark to find the *Blue Bell,* which by now had drifted three or four miles away. The two boats kept together by constant calling. But it was five in the afternoon of the next day before they found the vessel and were taken aboard. Mr. Paton saw members of the crew wearing his shirts and heard them boasting how they had bought them for a little tobacco, or gunpowder and caps. Since he now had only one shirt, he tried to get them to return one to him, but without success.

At Aneityum the missionaries were safely landed. Mr. Paton offered to pay the captain for having rescued them, but he refused to accept any money. The missionaries on the island did everything they could for the refugees. Mrs. Mathieson proved to be suffering from tuberculosis and within a month after landing, she fell asleep. Her husband, very depressed, succumbed only three months later.

"What are your plans now?" Dr. Geddie asked Mr. Paton shortly after he had arrived on Aneityum.

"I would like to remain here and proceed with my work of translating the Gospels. As soon as it is safe for me to do so, I intend to return to Tanna."

The other missionaries agreed that he should go to Australia. There he could visit the Presbyterian churches and tell them of the great need for workers in the New Hebrides. Especially should he try to raise money to buy a new mission ship for the work of the gospel in the New Hebrides. Another ship joining the *John Knox* in visiting the various mission stations regularly would prevent many of the terrible privations and risks such as Paton and the Mathiesons had suffered on Tanna.

Paton accepted the counsel of his brethren.

"I will go to Australia," he said. Dr. Geddie smiled.

"Very good. You can expect to sail for Australia in a few days."

IN PERIL AMONG FRIENDS

AT THE time it was decided that Paton should go to Australia, a trading ship was at Aneityum due to sail for Sydney in a few days. John paid the ten pounds charged as fare.

As baggage Paton had his Bible, and a collection of curios and idols which he planned to use to illustrate his talks in Australia. Before leaving Aneityum he bought a piece of cloth to make a shirt. The first thing he did on board ship was sit down and stitch the shirt together, for the only one he had was on his back. He had lost everything he owned on Tanna.

On board the ship were some natives who were brutally abused by the crew and the captain, who was a profane, hardened fellow. The way the natives were treated, and what he knew their fate would be, tore at the heart of Paton. Many times he found tears streaming down his cheeks as he was forced to witness the abuse.

They were compelled to work, but because they were from an island the language of which nobody on the ship understood, they were made to understand what was expected of them by cruel blows, and by being pushed or pulled here and there.

As soon as they were left alone they would sit on the deck and look pathetically and imploringly toward the sun. John decided they must be sun worshipers. How his heart ached to be able to tell them about the Sun of Righteousness.

During the voyage they were naked. Just before the ship reached Sydney each of them was given a piece of calico to wear as a kind of kilt.

When a government inspector boarded the trader at Sydney, he asked, "Who are those natives?"

"Oh, they are passengers," the captain answered, impudently.

No more questions were asked. But everybody, including the inspector, knew that they would be sold as slaves by the ship's captain.

During his last night on shipboard Paton walked the deck, anxiously wondering what would happen, and asking God to give him success in the job he had to do. The lights of Sydney through the darkness were a cheering sight. About midnight the ship dropped anchor in the harbor and waited for the dawn.

At first all doors in Sydney seemed to be closed to Paton. The ministers he met were sympathetic, but offered little help. After a week of disappointment things began to open up and soon he was speaking in large churches in the city.

People were thrilled as they listened to his story of mission life on Tanna. Purses were opened as he described the need for a mission boat to transport workers from island to island. When money began to come in, a committee was appointed to be responsible for it. Soon the fund began to climb—two hundred pounds, five hundred, a thousand pounds!

The visitor was given letters of introduction to ministers in other places, describing the bearer as a missionary from the South Seas and urging all Christians to give him help. Armed with this letter and his bag of curios, Paton set out to visit other cities, large and small, and many of the isolated hamlets of New South Wales, Victoria, and Tasmania.

The next months were among the most fascinating in Paton's life. Traveling by stagecoach, on foot, or in farm wagons, he found many warmhearted people who gladly contributed for the purchase of the *Dayspring*, the name Mr. Paton had decided to give the new ship.

In one small town a sheep farmer offered to pick up Paton and drive him to his home, where a meeting was planned. About noon they set out from a hotel. Riding in the farmer's buggy behind a pair of splendid black horses, they expected to reach their destination before dark.

They had been traveling about three hours, deep in conversation, when the man remarked, "We should soon be getting out of the bush and onto the plain."

But Mr. Paton was not so sure. He said to the driver, "These trees look very much like the ones we passed earlier in the afternoon."

The farmer laughed. "I am too old a hand in the bush for that! I have gone over this road many times before."

Paton made no reply. But almost immediately they saw the roof of the hotel through the trees, the very same hotel from which they had started at noon. The farmer looked around in amazement.

"Well, this beats all reckoning," he muttered, half to himself, half to his passenger. "I could have staked my life that this was impossible!"

They started out again. This time, by keeping a close watch on the path, the driver managed to get out of the woods and onto the plain, and finally arrived at his home, hours after the meeting was supposed to have been held.

For weeks Paton traveled from one ranch to another. Every donation received was mailed back to the committee in Sydney.

At one trading station the owner turned out to be a gruff Irishman who wanted nothing to do with the missionary.

"Go on! Go on!" he shouted. "I don't want to be troubled with the loikes o' you here."

Paton drove on down the road. But before he had gone far he heard a woman calling to the Irishman, "Please don't let the missionary go away. Tell him to come back. I want the children to see the idols and the other South Sea Island curios."

Paton continued on his way. But he heard the Irishman calling for him to stop, which he was glad to do. In a moment the man came up to the carriage. His voice had lost much of its gruffness. "The ladies and children wish to see your idols and your other curios. Will you please come back?"

Back Paton went, wondering how the women knew of him. It turned out that one of them had heard him speak in Melbourne. Now she was eager to have her sister see the curios. Paton was happy to spread his display before them. For fifteen minutes he described his work on the faraway islands. When he left, the Irishman handed him a check for five pounds and wished him success in his work.

It was not always easy for Paton to keep up with the schedule that had been outlined for him. Sometimes there was no transportation. One Friday night, at a place called Penola, he wondered how he was to get to the service advertised for the following evening at the home of a wealthy farmer living near Narracoort. The next morning a young woman offered a solution.

"I have a horse which I will gladly lend you for riding to Narracoort. He was a race horse when he was younger, so you should reach your destination very quickly. His name is Garibaldi."

Paton did not want to travel this way. Only once before had he ridden a horse, and he remembered that he had been sore for a week afterward. But every Australian in the bush country was perfectly at home on a horse, and it hardly occurred to them that others might have problems.

"But how would Garibaldi get back to you?" Paton asked.

"That's no problem," she replied. "I shall go fetch him myself."

Although he would rather have walked, Paton had to accept the woman's kind offer. There was no alternative.

The following morning, with no little misgiving, Paton mounted Garibaldi and set out for Narracoort, twenty-two miles away. A friend guided him to the edge of the village and started him on the right road.

"If you are unsure where you are going, just look for the notches that have been cut in the trees along the way," he told John as he bade him good-by.

After two or three miles Paton was joined by three men, also on horseback. They were amused at the way he rode in the saddle, and urged him to sit a little "freer." He tried, but explained that he was a novice. After a while they all noticed that the sky in the distance was beginning to darken.

"You had better ride a little faster," one man suggested. "It looks as though a heavy storm is coming."

But Paton had no desire to put his horse into a gallop. So bidding him good-by, the three set off at a gallop. This insulted Garibaldi, the one-time race horse. Feeling that his reputation was at stake, he suddenly laid back his ears, took the bit in his teeth, stretched out his long neck, and started galloping down the road at an appalling speed.

In a short time he caught up with the others and passed them at breakneck speed. The men then tried to keep up, but Garibaldi evidently had the idea that the pounding hoofs behind him were a challenge, so on he went, faster than ever, and soon left what he considered his competition far behind.

Then the rain began to fall—not a light sprinkle, but sheets that almost immediately soaked the rider. Every flash of lightning and every peal of thunder spurred Garibaldi to greater effort. The notches in the trees John was to follow were passed by in a blur. The path curved this way and that, and at every turn Paton expected to be dashed against some giant of the forest. His high hat, now out of shape by the rain, he pushed down over his head to prevent its being carried away. He was plastered with mud, but the horse kept on.

Garibaldi covered the miles in record time. And at last,

6

With the bit in his teeth, Garabaldi galloped at breakneck
speed through the night, which was lit only by lightning
flashes.

through an opening in the forest, Paton saw the road slope down a long decline. He glimpsed a farmhouse—his destination—at the bottom of the valley.

Evidently Garibaldi had been there before, for he headed straight for the stables. Paton fully expected to be dashed to death against the barn door. His every attempt to slow the horse by pulling back on the bridle was in vain; Garibaldi continued galloping onward.

Members of the family, who had been watching for the missionary, rushed out onto the front porch, and they were appalled to see the horse charging down the hill with the rider either unable or unwilling to slow him down. A groom also saw the danger. He ran into the path of the charging animal and seized the reins. By running beside the horse, holding back with all his might, he finally stopped him a few feet from the barn.

"I have saved your life," shouted the groom to Paton. "What madness to ride like that!" The whole family ran over from the porch—father, mother, and five children.

"Thank you, thank you," murmured Mr. Paton, trying to catch his breath. He well knew that they would scarcely believe him to be their expected visitor. His clothing was covered with mud and water. His hat was battered all out of shape. He also knew what they were thinking—that he was drunk! As if to convince them that this was so, when he finally managed to slip out of the saddle he collapsed into a heap on the ground, his head still whirling from the mad race. When he finally staggered to his feet he had to hold onto the veranda to stand. Embarrassed beyond words, for the next few moments he didn't even try to say anything.

Finally the farmer said, "Won't you come in?" and John made his way, swaying, into the house, where he sat before a warm fire.

"Wouldn't you like to change your clothes?" asked the farmer.

"Yes, I would, but my bags are coming on the cart and may not be here tonight."

The farmer then led Paton to a bedroom, spread out one of his own suits on the bed, and left Paton to put it on. Since the farmer was a large man, above average in height, and Paton was short and thin, he looked very strange in his new attire.

"Have you arranged for a meeting?" Paton asked.

The farmer spoke up, almost reprovingly.

"Do you really consider yourself fit to appear before a congregation?"

Paton smiled.

"I know what you are thinking. But you are wrong. I have never touched a drop of liquor in my life. It was that horseback ride that upset me."

In a little while they gathered around the supper table. The family could scarcely conceal their amusement when they saw Paton dressed in the farmer's suit. Their surreptitious glances told him they still thought he was drunk.

Again he tried to explain.

"Dear friends," he said, "I am quite aware of your feelings and understand them perfectly. Appearances are against me. But I am not drunk as you suppose. I am a lifelong teetotaler."

This fairly broke them down. They laughed and looked at one another, then back at the missionary as much as to say, "You're drunk this very moment."

Before supper was finished, however, they began to think that he might be able to conduct a meeting. Of course once the meeting started and Paton began relating his experiences in the South Sea Islands, all their doubts were swept away. From then on they heaped kindness upon him. When he left they gave him a liberal offering for his ship and begged his forgiveness for their failure to be more hospitable when he first arrived.

The following morning the groom led Garibaldi out of the barn, saddled him, and with another horse in tow, rode off to return him to his owner. The horse was apparently none the worse for wear. Paton could not say the same of himself, for he felt the effects of that ride for several weeks. His hat was never the same again.

In after years Paton twice visited this farm. On each occasion the lady of the house amused her guests with a vivid description of the manner in which the missionary had first arrived at her door.

After having traveled over much of eastern Australia, Paton returned to Sydney to report on his work and to learn how the ship fund was progressing. To his delight he was told that some five thousand pounds had been raised. It was planned that three thousand would be sent to Nova Scotia, Canada, where a new mission ship would be built.

Paton's plan was to return at once to the islands and preach the gospel. But his brethren in Sydney had other ideas.

"Brother Paton," said the presiding elder, laying a hand on his shoulder, "you have collected money for the ship. But suppose the ship has no one to carry to the islands. We need missionaries even more desperately than we need a ship. Now that you have collected the money, we must look to you to find the men for her to carry.

"We are agreed that in Scotland you will find the men and women to man those island missions. Return to your homeland, visit your parents, then stir up the home churches to send us some consecrated men."

Impressed that this was God's will for him, Paton agreed to go.

Four weeks later he boarded the *Kosciusko,* bound for London and home.

BACK TO THE SOUTH SEAS

JOHN PATON sat in his compartment of the train from London and looked through the rainswept windows at the green Scottish countryside. A tedious voyage of more than three months had brought him from Australia to England. Now he was in his own beloved Scotland once more.

Having reported to the convener of the Foreign Mission Committee at Castle Douglas, he caught another train for Dumfries. At Dumfries he boarded a stagecoach for Torthorwald, about five miles away. From there he walked the mile to the cottage where his aged parents still lived. A thousand memories crowded his mind as he walked the familiar road. His parents gave him a joyful welcome, mixed with sadness, since his wife, Janet, was not with him.

A few days later it was Paton's painful duty to call on his wife's parents. As sincere Christians they had accepted the death of their daughter and grandson as permitted by the Lord. With tears falling fast, Father Robson took Paton's hand and said, "When you left, had I known what I know now, I would still have gladly given my daughter to the work of God."

It was exciting for Paton to meet many friends of years gone by. He also had long conferences with the leaders of his mission society. Soon he was on the road again, visiting Presbyterian churches throughout the country. Everywhere he pleaded the cause of missions, and he received generous contributions for the support of the new overseas workers he hoped to find.

To the Scottish boys and girls Paton made a special appeal. Adults had contributed money to buy the *Dayspring* (the name the new mission ship was to bear), and would it not be a splendid project for the boys and girls to raise money to keep the ship traveling among the islands? The children did not disappoint him. Boxes were placed in many church vestries. Into them went the pennies of the children of Scotland.

One day Paton received good news from the mission board. Four young volunteers had offered to go to the South Sea Islands from Scotland, and three from Nova Scotia.

John took a new wife with him when he returned to the South Seas. A young woman, Margaret Whitecross, whose whole family was interested in mission work, and whose brother had died in a far-off mission field, seemed in every respect to be the kind of wife he needed. They were married in her sister's house in Edinburgh.

Before the day of departure Paton made one last visit to Torthorwald to bid farewell to his godly parents. Once more they knelt together. With many tears Father Paton committed his dear children to the Lord's care and called down Heaven's richest blessing upon them. John Paton had a premonition that he would not see his parents again on earth, so this parting was a particularly poignant one.

In what was then considered a fast passage, ninety-five days, the ship with the missionaries embarked from Liverpool and sailed to Sydney. The *Dayspring* had already arrived in Australia from Canada. Although she was fully paid for, there was not enough money to operate her. At first this financial problem was a great concern to Paton. But then warm friends came to the rescue with donations just when they were needed.

Later in the year Mr. and Mrs. Paton sailed on the *Dayspring* for a tour of the islands, during which they stopped at

Aneityum to attend a general meeting.

During their tour they visited some islands controlled by the French. They found that mission work was hampered there by the anti-missionary attitude of the authorities. At first Protestant missionaries had been kept out, but when Great Britain protested, some had been allowed to enter. The work was difficult because all communication had to be in French.

On one island some Protestant parents asked Mr. Paton to conduct worship and baptize some children. Paton knew that were he to ask permission to baptize, it would be refused, but he felt that he could not decline to obey the command of Jesus. News of what he had done quickly reached the French authorities. In two days the private secretary of the Governor came to see him with an interpreter.

"Is it true that you have been baptizing here?"

"It is true."

"By whose authority?"

"By the authority of my Great Master."

"When did you get that authority?"

"When I was licensed and ordained to preach the gospel!"

The secretary bowed politely and the two men left. Paton had no further trouble there.

While the Patons had been on Aneityum for the general meetings, a British man-of-war, the H.M.S. *Curacoa,* had arrived to investigate the circumstances surrounding the murder of the Gordons on Erromanga and other complaints regarding incidents on other islands. A British baronet, Sir William Wiseman, was in charge of the investigation. While discussing the matter with the missionaries Sir William said to Paton, "I understand that you speak the Tannese language quite well."

"Yes, sir," replied the missionary.

"Will you go with me to Tanna? I need a translator."

Paton agreed to go, and a few days later the *Curacoa* sailed into the harbor of Port Resolution. Sir William called the most important chiefs and told them the reason for his visit. Through Paton he said that missionaries, traders, and natives would be punished alike if they disturbed the peace. "Now, I want you to bring me the men who 'tried to kill' the missis, and who stole their things," he said.

The chiefs shuffled guiltily, but none said anything. And in spite of Sir William's persistence, none volunteered any information.

"Then I shall have to punish you by destroying some of your villages," said Sir William. "Leave your villages, for we shall destroy two tomorrow. Go to Nowar's land. There you will be safe."

As the hour approached for the shelling of the two villages, hundreds of defiant Tannese warriors gathered on the beach, shaking their spears and muskets, foolishly determined to fight the man-of-war. Sir William commanded the sailors to load the guns. Orders were given to fire into the side of the hill underneath the warriors.

A cannon roared. A shell exploded into the hillside, throwing earth and shattered bush into the air around the dancing, defiant men.

The whole army turned and raced through the trees for the safety of Nowar's land. Two shells were sent over their heads, exploding with a terrific roar and thoroughly scaring them.

Two villages were shelled. No lives were lost. A similar visit was made to Erromanga and punishment meted out.

The story of these events quickly spread throughout the islands. The heathen at last agreed that it was bad to murder the whites and steal from them.

Back on Aneityum the Patons wondered where they should settle. John wished to return to Tanna, but the other missionaries felt that it would be unwise. Fifteen or twenty miles northeast of Tanna lay a much smaller island, Aniwa. The missionary family was invited to begin work there.

When moving the Patons from Aneityum to Aniwa, the *Dayspring* stopped at Port Resolution and had to stay there

89

for several days because of bad weather. The Tannese were amazed to see the beautiful new mission ship and to learn that more missionaries were settling on various islands.

"How does it happen?" they asked. "We kill them, rob them, and drive them away. If anyone treated us like that, nobody would ever persuade us to return! Yet here they are in a beautiful ship with many more missis!"

Meanwhile a host of memories, some happy and some sad, crowded into Paton's mind as the *Dayspring* sailed into Port Resolution.

Soon word got around that Missi Paton was on the ship. One afternoon a canoe put out from the shore and approached the ship. As it drew near, Paton saw that it was manned by Nowar and his men. The old chief drew his canoe up beside the vessel and climbed aboard. He asked the captain for the missionary's boxes.

"I'm sorry, but I can't give them to you," replied the captain. "Missi Paton is going somewhere else. I am not allowed to land his boxes on Tanna."

"You don't need to land them," replied the wily chief. "I will arrange everything for Missi. Just throw them over the side; my men will catch every box before it reaches the water and carry them all safely ashore."

"Can't be done," replied the captain again.

Nowar then appealed to the missionary.

"Missi Paton, will you not come ashore with me? I am sure that Missi Paton the woman will be glad to see the site of your house."

To humor the old man, the two went ashore. Nowar led them to the spot where John Paton's house had been built. Now nothing was left of it. Paton visited his wife's grave, now overgrown with weeds. Then they went to Nowar's village. The chief led them to his extensive plantations. Turning eagerly to Mrs. Paton, he remarked, "See, plenty of food! While I have a yam or a banana, you shall not want."

But Mrs. Paton replied calmly, "I fear no lack of food."

He pointed them to some of his warriors standing nearby.

"We are many! We are strong! We can always protect you."

"I am not afraid," replied Mrs. Paton.

In one last attempt to persuade her to remain on Tanna, Nowar led her to the large tree in which John Paton had spent a long night, wondering if he would see another sunrise. At Nowar's request Paton described to his wife what had happened in that tree. Then, with obviously genuine feeling the old chief declared, "The God who protected Missi will always protect you."

Again she said that she was not afraid. Then she explained that, for the present, they would go to Aniwa. Perhaps some time the Lord would open the way for them to return to Tanna.

Poor Nowar was defeated. Sadly he walked with the Patons to the boat that carried them to the *Dayspring*.

Several years later the Patons discovered that Nowar had done something very special for them. While the Patons were making their short visit to Tanna, a sacred man from Aniwa was also visiting there. Nowar talked with him about Missi Paton and his wife, who were going to settle on Aniwa. From his arm Nowar took some white shells that were emblems of his chieftainship, and bound them around the arm of the sacred man.

"By these shells," Nowar solemnly declared, "you promise to protect my missi and his wife and child on Aniwa. If any evil comes to them, I warn you, by this pledge, that I and my people will avenge in full the injury done to them." This oath was not forgotten.

That same evening the *Dayspring* sailed from Tanna. God never guided Paton back to that dark island, but he lived to see other missionaries settle there. Before he finally left for his homeland, hundreds of Tannese had become Christians.

The little island of Aniwa, on which the Patons now landed, was only seven miles long by two miles wide. The highest point on the island was hardly more than a high mound. The soil was so sandy that when rain fell, most of the moisture quickly disappeared.

There is no harbor or safe anchorage on Aniwa, which makes it inconvenient for trading ships to stop. A small boat lowered from the *Dayspring* brought Paton, his wife, and their tiny son to the island. The islanders received them kindly, carrying their supplies to a large hut prepared for them by Aneityumese teachers settled on the island. They would live there until John was able to build a permanent house.

The hut was a one-room, reed and leaf structure. It had no doors or windows, only open places in the walls. Paton screened off a small part for their bed. The other was used for church services on Sundays and as a schoolroom on weekdays. The children came there every morning for reading class, which was conducted by the Aneityumese teachers. The Patons' only furniture was the boxes in which they had brought their goods. One of them served as a crib for baby Paton.

From the sad experience with malaria on Tanna, Paton knew better than to build his house down on the beach. After looking around for a while, he found a place he liked about half a mile inland on the island's highest rise. But for some reason known only to the islanders, they refused him permission to build there. They led him to another place not quite so high and closer to the shore and informed him he could build on that spot. In his hut John opened one of his boxes and brought out hatchets, blankets, nails, beads, and other items the islanders loved. With these he purchased the land for his house.

Early the next morning John and his helpers went up the hill to begin work. At the top were mounds that had to be removed to prepare the foundation for the house. In the mounds were many human bones. Paton knew now that this place had once been the scene of cannibal feasts. With two baskets filled with bones, John asked a chief who was watching what was going on, "What are these bones doing here?"

The chief shrugged his shoulders eloquently, and replied, "Ah, we are not Tanna men. We do not eat the bones!"

One day while John was building the door frames of his house, he found that he needed some nails and tools. He picked up a piece of smooth wood and wrote on it what he wanted. He handed this to the old chief, who happened to be watching, and asked him to take the wood to his wife and return with the things needed.

"But what do you want?" asked the chief.

"Never mind. The wood will tell her."

A puzzled look came over the old man's face.

"What does Missi mean? Who ever heard of wood speaking?"

"Try it and see what happens," replied Mr. Paton with a smile.

Greatly mystified, the chief started out on what he thought would be a fruitless errand. At the hut Mrs. Paton read her husband's message and quickly brought out the items he had asked for. The old chief ran all the way back to the new house and demanded an explanation of the miracle. When Paton had explained it, the chief was thrilled, and wondered whether he could ever learn to read the speaking wood.

Paton often wondered why the people of Aniwa had forbidden him the first site he chose, but had been quite willing to let him build on another. Three years later, when Chief Namakei became a Christian, he made an eloquent speech to his own people. In that speech Paton found the answer to his question.

"When Missi came we saw his boxes," the chief said. "We knew he had blankets and calico, axes and knives, fishhooks and all such things. We said, 'Don't drive him away, else we will lose all these things. We will sell him land, but we will force him to live on the sacred plot. Our gods

The old chief was mystified. "How can wood speak? Who ever
heard of wood speaking?"

will kill him, and we will divide all that he has among the men of Aniwa.'

"So Missi built his house on our most sacred spot. He and his people lived there, and the gods did not strike. He planted bananas there, and we said, 'Now when they eat those bananas they will all drop dead,' as our fathers assured us would happen to anyone who ate fruit from that ground, except our sacred men themselves.

"The bananas ripened and they ate them. We watched for days and days, but no one died! Therefore what we say, and what our fathers have said, is not true. Our gods cannot kill them. Their Jehovah God is stronger than the gods of Aniwa."

Paton smiled. At last he knew why he had been given the second-best site on Aniwa. By simply living there, he had been preaching a sermon about the strength of his Jehovah God!

LIGHT OVERCOMING DARKNESS

WHEN the Patons began their work on Aniwa, there were two Aneityumese Christian teachers and their wives already on the island. But other than that the contrast of their godly lives may have made some impression on the Aniwanese, no results of their work was apparent. The people came to the services, but only because afterward they were given food. Paton put an end to this practice, and for a time most of the islanders stayed away. The ones who came were genuinely interested.

In every way he could Paton tried to show his love for the islanders. He learned that there were many orphaned children on the island, some of whose relatives took little interest in them. So he built cottages and brought the neglected ones to live in them. Next he built a schoolhouse and began to teach the children. Every Sunday these orphans went to church, clothed in neat dresses or pants. This delighted the islanders. Again, as the relatives listened to the orphans, and saw how they were learning so much, they became much more willing to listen. Soon parents brought their own children to Mr. Paton and asked him to teach them also.

The first child to be entrusted to the Patons was the daughter of Namakei, who befriended the missionaries as Chief Nowar had done on Tanna. Namakei often visited the missionaries in their home and helped Paton learn the language of the island. Sometimes he brought his wife and other chiefs to talk with the Patons. In time, they began to ask about the God whose home was in the sky.

So one morning Namakei came to Paton with his only child, whose mother was dead. Placing his hands on her small shoulders he looked the kind missionary in the face.

"I want to leave Litsi with you," he said. "I want you to train her for Jesus."

And so the Patons had their first pupil, Litsi Soré. Her name meant Litsi the Great, for she could become queen of her race someday. Litsi was a clever child, and she became a great help to Mrs. Paton. Before long Namakei's younger brother, a sacred man who had once tried to shoot Mr. Paton, brought his child too. Her mother was also dead. Her name was Litsi Sisi, or Litsi the Little, and she too helped the missionaries and soon learned how to read.

On Aniwa, as on most tropical islands, there were many sick people. Paton had brought certain medicines with him to treat some of their diseases, and often the people came to him for help. One morning a local chief came for medicine. But Paton was busy, and could not help him at once. At this the chief, enraged, strode off into the jungle, muttering to himself, "I will be revenged. I must be attended to. I won't wait for *him!*" But before long he realized that he needed medicine more than revenge.

On another occasion John became the target for the vengeance of a young chief, Youwili, because he broke a taboo Youwili had set. One morning while Paton was clearing bush around the mission house Youwili suddenly appeared out of the bush, and threatingly commanded him to stop. Not wishing to quarrel, Paton obeyed. Then with his tomahawk Youwili cut down part of the fence in front of the house, as well as two or three banana trees John had planted. From where he stood, Paton saw Chief Namakei and some of his men looking anxiously at what Youwili was doing. Before he left, Youwili shook his club, intimating that he needed only a further excuse to kill John. Then he stalked off into the

With his ax, Youwili chopped down all of the fence Paton
had built.

bush. Namakei and his companions came to speak with Paton.

"Missi, do you know what Youwili's action means? It means he has declared war on you."

"Well, if you let him act this way, perhaps you do not want us any longer on Aniwa. If this is not corrected, I shall remain in my house until the mission ship arrives. Then we can sail on it to some other island where we will be protected."

Now that the islanders had begun to love their missionaries, this was a powerful argument. Paton went into the house and shut the door. Soon the house was surrounded by a crowd of men and women pleading through the windows for the Patons not to leave. Mr. Paton went out to talk with them.

"You know our resolution," he said, "and it is for you to decide. Either you control that foolish young man or we will go."

Many speeches were made. At last the chief came to the door and spoke.

"We have decided to punish this foolish young man. But when we have caught him, we will bring him here. Please tell us what to do with him. Shall we kill him?"

"Certainly not," replied the missionary. "Only for murder can life be lawfully taken."

"Then shall we burn his house and destroy his plantations?"

"No."

"Shall we bind him and beat him?"

"No."

"Shall we put him into a canoe and push him out into the sea to drown or to be eaten by sharks?"

"No, by no means!"

"Missi, these are our only ways of punishing people who misbehave. Tell us then, what shall we do?"

"Make him, with his own hands and with no help from anyone, build a new fence and restore everything he has destroyed. Also, he must promise publicly that his evil conduct toward us will cease. That will satisfy us."

The people laughed and cheered, thinking it a great joke to make Youwili repair the fence he had destroyed. After considerable searching, Youwili's hiding place in the bush was found, and he was taken before the assembly of his own people. Youwili trembled, for he knew he could be killed. When the council told him that the sentence was to repair the fence and promise to stop fighting Missi he was greatly relieved, and agreed.

"Tomorrow," said Youwili slowly, "I will fully restore the fence. Never again will I oppose Missi. His word is good."

True to his word, Youwili was at work early next morning, rebuilding the broken fence. By evening everything was snug and actually better than it had been before. While Youwili was working, some young fellows came by and twitted him about the affair.

"Youwili," they said, "you find it much easier to cut down Missi's fence than to repair it. You will not repeat that in a hurry."

Youwili listened in silence. When others came by with their faces turned away, he knew they were laughing at him. When the job was finished, he left without saying a word to Mr. Paton. The missionary had been tempted to go and work with young Youwili, but he decided it would be better to leave him to do his own task. Therefore, his prayers ascended daily that the Spirit would speak to Youwili's heart and convert him.

One morning Paton, helped by two boys, was pulling a cartload of coral blocks up from the seashore. The load was heavy, and he was sweating. Suddenly Youwili came running down the hill, shouting, "Missi, that work is too hard for you. Let me be your helper."

He stepped between the shafts and with the help of the two boys, pulled, it seemed, with the strength of a horse, and got the cart to the top of the hill. John Paton followed, with tears of joy in his eyes, for now he felt sure that Youwili was ready to accept the yoke of Christ.

One year, because of prolonged drought, food became very scarce. The orphans often went to bed hungry. One day they said to Mr. Paton, "Missi, we do not have enough food. We wish we could have some of the white man's biscuits."

"We all do not have enough food, dear children," Mr. Paton replied, "but when the *Dayspring* arrives we shall have enough. When it does you shall have biscuits again."

Still the children lingered. Finally an older boy spoke up.

"Missi, you have two beautiful fig trees. Will you let us have a feast on the tender young leaves?"

"Gladly, my children, take your fill."

In a twinkling each child was perched on a high branch, feasting contentedly on fig leaves.

Every morning the children scanned the vast sea surrounding their little island, then came back to their "father," saying sadly, "Missi, no vessel yet."

But one glad day their words were changed.

"The vessel! Hurrah!"

Everybody hurried down to the beach. Sure enough, there was a vessel, but what ship was it?

"It's not the *Dayspring*," said the children, "for the *Dayspring* has two masts, and this vessel has three." Paton was to learn soon that their beautiful mission ship had struck a reef and been lost.

Through his telescope Paton saw boxes and barrels being put over the side of the ship into a smaller boat. Within an hour the little boat was at the coral dock. Eager hands carried or rolled the boxes and barrels up the hill.

"Missi," cried one of the orphans, "here is a cask that rattles like biscuits! Will you let us take it to the mission house?"

"Of course, my children."

They soon had the barrel rolling up the path to the mission. When he returned home, Paton found the children standing around the barrel.

"Missi," they asked a little anxiously, "have you forgotten your promise?"

"Forgotten what?" he asked, a twinkle in his eye.

The children began whispering to one another. "Missi has forgotten."

"What are you talking about?" he asked again, trying to keep a straight face.

"Missi, you promised that when the vessel came you would give us each a biscuit."

"Oh," laughed Paton, "I didn't forget. I just wanted to see if you would remember."

"No fear of that, Missi. Will you open the cask soon? We are dying for biscuits."

With hammer and chisel he knocked off the hoops, then gave each child one biscuit. To his surprise they just stood there. No one started to eat.

"What!" he exclaimed, "you are dying for biscuits, but you don't eat? Are you expecting another?"

The oldest child spoke up. "We must first thank God for sending us food and ask Him to bless it."

After they had given thanks in their own simple way, the biscuits disappeared quickly.

AN ISLAND ELOPEMENT

AS TIME went on John decided that his house was too small, so he set about to add a couple of rooms. While he was working on the foundations he noticed an armed savage lurking nearby every day, watching him work. The man had a bad reputation, for he had killed another man shortly before the Patons arrived on Aniwa. A little worried about his intentions, Paton spoke to him.

"Nelwang, do you have words for me?"

"Yes, Missi, if you will only help me now, I will be your friend forever."

"Of course I will help you. That is why I am here and why I remain."

"Yes; but I want you to be strong as my friend, and I will be strong for you."

"Well, tell me how I can help you."

"I want to get married, and I need your help."

"Nelwang," replied the missionary seriously, "you know that marriages here are arranged in childhood. I would not dare to interfere in such matters. Do you want to bring trouble on me and my family? It might cost us our lives."

"Oh, Missi, you don't understand. The circumstances are very different."

"It shouldn't be complicated. If you find a woman who loves you and you love her, go ahead and marry her."

"Yes, but this is where the trouble comes in. You see, I want to marry Yakin, the widow of one of the island chiefs. That will break no infant betrothals."

"Are you sure she loves you?"

"Of course she loves me. She met me one day on the path. I told her I wanted to marry her, and she slipped off her earrings and handed them to me. If she loved another more she would have given them to him."

"If that is true, then why don't you marry her?"

"Well, you see, here is my difficulty. In her village are thirty young bachelors. Each of them would like to marry Yakin, but if one of them takes her, the other twenty-nine will shoot him."

"Then," said the missionary, "if you take her, I suppose the thirty disappointed bachelors will shoot you. Is that what is worrying you?"

"Exactly. And that is where I need your help. Let me tell you my plan and see if you think it will work."

Mr. Paton listened and gave some advice. That night Nelwang stationed two of his friends at each end of Yakin's village to warn him if they saw anyone coming. Then with his tomahawk he cut through the fence behind Yakin's house. A few whispers in the dark, and the bride-to-be followed her would-be husband into the thick bush where they could hide until they found some better place to go.

The following morning the hole in the fence behind Yakin's house was discovered, and investigation showed that she was gone.

After a little investigating, the thirty disappointed suitors discovered that Nelwang also had disappeared. They then rushed to his house and either destroyed or took all his property. The same was done to Yakin's house, which was the usual way of taking revenge under the circumstances. Feasting, dancing, and shouting went on as the men comforted themselves at the expense of the missing couple.

Three weeks passed, and Paton wondered what had become of Nelwang and his bride. Everybody believed they had gone by canoe to Tanna or Erromanga. But suddenly one morning as John was working on his house Nelwang appeared at his side.

"Hello!" Paton exclaimed. "Where did you come from? Where is Yakin?"

"I can't tell you exactly. It is a secret. We live on coconuts that we gather at night. We want to come and stay with you until peace is made. May we come tomorrow?"

"All right," Paton replied, "come, both of you."

The news that the newlyweds were with the missionaries traveled very quickly. Nelwang followed Mr. Paton everywhere he went, and Yakin stuck close to Mrs. Paton. Yakin was shown a missionary barrel that had recently arrived, and was invited to clothe herself in any garments she could find that would fit her.

"Nelwang," said the missionary one Saturday, "I think it is time for you to come to church and let the people know that you are really husband and wife. The people must accept what has happened."

"Very good, Missi, we will come tomorrow."

Nelwang knew the customs of the mission. When the bell stopped ringing everyone was supposed to be seated, men on one side and women on the other.

On Sunday morning, just after the bell ceased ringing, Nelwang entered the building, grasping his tomahawk fiercely in his hand. He marched to the front of the church and sat down.

Through the door appeared a strange-looking Yakin. In the islands when a person began wearing clothes it was a sign he had become a Christian. Yakin was determined that no one should doubt her Christianity. She was a walking mass of rags, with both men's and women's clothing draped over her body.

The day was hot. The preacher gazed down in pity on that poor bride, sweltering before him. He cut the service short; probably it was the shortest sermon John Paton had ever preached!

From then on, Yakin continued to be Mrs. Paton's helper. She learned to read and write, and became an excellent Sunday school teacher. Nelwang became Mr. Paton's faithful bodyguard. Truly he and Yakin were new creatures in Jesus Christ. The old things in their lives had truly passed away.

A WELL OF WATER

JUST when things seemed to be going well for the little Christian band on Aniwa, Satan decided to stir up trouble. One old chief, who had once been friendly to Paton, suddenly for no apparent reason turned against him.

While the islanders were entering church one Sunday morning, this old chief brought all his material near the church and, with every effort to catch the people's attention, began to make a canoe. A short time later he became sick and died.

His brother took up the controversy and came to the meetinghouse with a group of armed warriors. He boldly challenged the Christians to fight, but they refused. Then he went up to one of the Christians and struck him with his club. The man fell back a step or two, but he refused to strike back.

"I shall leave my revenge to Jehovah," he said meekly. The heathen party were disgusted. They left, their hopes for a fight frustrated.

A few days later this brother of the chief also fell sick and suddenly died. The heathen were enraged and summoned a council of everyone on the island who did not like the Jehovah worship. The meeting lasted for hours. They agreed among themselves that the Missi must either be killed or forced to leave Aniwa.

Then a sacred man arose and walked slowly to the front.

"When I was on Tanna, a man-of-war came and punished the thieves and murderers on that island by shelling their villages. I will never forget the damage done by the big guns on that warship."

His voice became even more serious as he continued, "Nowar, the great chief of Port Resolution, tried to persuade Missi and his wife to stay on Tanna. When he saw this could not be done, he took these shells from his arm. They are tokens of his own chieftainship. He bound them to my arm and made me promise that I would protect Missi and his wife from all harm. He told me to tell the men of Aniwa that if the Missi were injured or killed, he and his warriors would come from Tanna and take full revenge in blood."

A quietness fell over the assembly. The evil plan was abandoned, and with no further discussion the men returned to their villages.

One Sunday morning not long after, the heathen marched past the church, chanting, on their way to go fishing, at the same time threatening to ambush Paton and his native teachers when they traveled to other villages. Paton realized that this challenge had to be met, so he invited all the Christian men to come to his house the next morning. "From there," Paton said, "we will all go together to see if we can reason with these heathen."

After worship and breakfast next morning, Paton stepped out to find nearly eighty warriors waiting to escort him to the heathen village. He was disappointed to see that they were carrying weapons, which they flatly refused to leave behind. Rather than go alone, Paton reluctantly allowed them to accompany him, armed as they were.

The heathen were astonished when they saw the strength of the Christian party. The talking lasted all day. Paton found it endlessly wearisome, but he was glad it was words the men were using against one another rather than spears. Before returning to the mission, Paton obtained a promise from the heathen party that from henceforth they would leave the worship alone and not molest the believers or disturb the meetings in any way. Paton, tired but happy, lay down to sleep that night with the words "Blessed are the peacemakers" going through his mind.

This occurrence helped a great deal to strengthen the roots of Christianity, but it was the digging of the well that did the most to break the back of heathenism.

The rainy season on Aniwa lasted only from December to April. Even then, the water seeped into the light soil and was lost, as we noted previously. Thus, often there was little water remaining during the last month of the dry season. At such times coconut milk was a liquid treasure.

The natives were accustomed to little water, and could make out, although they greatly appreciated an ample supply of fresh water. The Paton household found the lack very difficult. So John decided to dig a well. He realized that, even after it was dug, the water, if he found any, might be salty. But he would try anyway, trusting that God would help.

One morning, when Chief Namakei and another chief came to talk to Paton about the religion of Jehovah, Paton said to them, "I am going to dig a deep hole in the earth to see if my God will send us fresh water from below."

The chiefs were astonished. To them the very idea was absurd.

"Oh, Missi!" exclaimed Namakei in tones of concerned pity. "Wait till the rain comes down. We will save you all we possibly can."

But Missi did not feel that he could wait.

"We may all die for lack of water sometime when the rain fails to come. If no fresh water can be found, we may be forced to leave you."

Namakei looked at the white man imploringly. "Oh, Missi! You must not leave us for that. But rain comes only from above. How could you expect our island to send us showers of rain from below?"

"In my country fresh water does come springing up out of the ground. I hope it will do the same here."

Chief Namakei then exclaimed, "Missi, your head is going wrong; you are losing something or you would not talk wild like that! Don't let our people hear you talking about going down into the earth for rain, or they will never listen to your words or believe you again."

Paton refused to be discouraged. Having chosen what he thought was a promising site, he brought out his pick and shovel and began to dig. The chief, convinced that John had gone out of his mind, instructed some of his men to remain near and watch, fearing that Missi might try to take his own life or do something equally outrageous.

"Poor Missi!" he said sadly. "That's the way with everyone who goes mad. There is no driving a notion out of their heads. We must watch him now. He will find it harder to work with pick and spade than to write books and preach in church. Then when he's tired maybe he will give it up."

Toiling under the hot sun, Paton did indeed find the work much harder than he had expected. But he refused to be defeated. However, deciding that the job was too much for himself alone, he went into his house and filled a pocket with beautifully made English fishhooks, so superior to hooks the natives used, even though they were cleverly made of shell and bone. Paton held up one of the hooks for all to see.

"One of these will be given to every man who digs, fills, and empties three full bucketloads of dirt out of that hole."

There was a rush for bucket and spade. Taking turns, the men worked for hours. Fishhooks disappeared like magic, but the hole went down very slowly. Nevertheless, when the sun set and the men quit for the night, the well was twelve feet deep.

But the next morning, when Paton went to continue work on the well, he was dismayed to see that during the night one side had caved in and much of the work would have to be done over. Now Chief Namakei was more concerned than ever. He pointed to the damage and told Paton he was being very foolish. For the fiftieth time he assured the missionary that rain would never come from the earth on Aniwa.

"And," he continued, driving home his position with all the eloquence at his command, "that's not all. If you had been in that hole last night, you would have been buried. Then a man-of-war would come from Queen 'Toria to ask for the Missi that lives here. We would say, 'He's down in that hole.'

"The captain would ask, 'Who killed him and put him down there?' We would have to say, 'He went down there himself!' The captain would answer, 'Nonsense. Who ever heard of a man going down into the earth to bury himself? You killed him, you put him down there; don't try to hide your bad conduct with lies.'

"Then he would bring out his big guns and shoot us and destroy our island. You are making your own grave, Missi, and you will make ours too. Give up this mad idea, for no rain will be found by going downward on Aniwa! Besides, all your fishhooks cannot tempt my men again to enter that hole; they don't want to be buried with you. Will you give it up now?"

Paton did what he could to calm the old man's fears. But he was determined with God's help to sink that well. In order to lift the dirt, he rigged up a windlass with a rope going down into the deepening hole. When he had filled a bucket, he would ring a little bell and the natives would pull the bucket to the top, dump the dirt, and lower the bucket once more. But not one of them would go into the hole. Hour after hour Paton toiled away, occasionally coming to the top, quite exhausted. As the days went by, the well grew deeper. Finally it had gone down thirty feet and still no water. John's heart began to sink about as deep as the well.

But as he determinedly dug away at the earth, the phrase "living water" kept running through his mind. He was not ready to give up.

A little past the thirty-foot depth John noticed that the sand was beginning to feel damp; he knew that water was near. But the great question was, Will it be fresh or salty? That evening he tried to encourage the chief.

Paton dipped his cup into the water. The chief was about to receive the surprise of his life.

"I think my Jehovah God will give me water tomorrow from that hole."

Chief Namakei threw a pitying glance at his friend and shook his head.

"No, Missi, you will never see rain coming up from the earth on this island. We wonder what is to be the end of this mad work of yours. We expect daily, if you reach water, to see you drop through into the sea, and the sharks will eat you. That will be the end of it; death to you, and danger to us all."

Paton persisted. "Come tomorrow. I hope and believe that God will send rain water up through the earth." He realized that he might be disappointed, but somehow he had faith to believe that God would hear and answer his prayer.

Next morning, at daybreak, John went down into the well. Already the natives had gathered to see what would happen. Trembling with excitement, he sank a narrow hole about two feet, in the center of the well. Immediately water rushed up and began to fill the hole. Cupping his trembling hands, he scooped up some of the muddy liquid and eagerly tasted it. Overwhelming joy filled his heart. He dropped to his knees in the mud to praise the Lord. It was fresh water!

John had taken a small cup down the well with him. Filling it with water, he called up, "You can bring me up now."

The men had seen Paton take the empty cup into the well. Now he handed it to the astonished chief. The chief took it and looked at the water. Then he shook it to see if it would spill, and touched it to see if it felt like water. Finally he took a mouthful, rolled it around in his mouth for a few seconds, then swallowed it. His astonishing shout rang out.

"Rain! Rain! Yes, it is rain! But how did you get it?"

"My Jehovah God sent it to me out of His own earth in answer to our prayers and labors. Go, look down and see the water for yourselves."

The very thought gave the chief and all his men the shivers. Every man there could fearlessly climb to the top of the highest coconut palm, but not one dared peer down into the hole. Finally they made a plan. They would hold each other's hands tightly, and form a line. The man in front would look down, then take his place at the end of the line until all had seen the water at the bottom of the well.

When the chief's turn came, he could not contain his astonishment. "Missi, wonderful, wonderful is the work of your Jehovah God. No god of Aniwa ever helped us in this way. But Missi, will this water always be there? Or will it be like the rain that comes and goes?"

"I think it will always be there."

"Will it be just for you and your family, or may we also have a little now and then?"

"I believe there will be enough for us all. You may have water from this hole any time you need it."

Old Chief Namakei looked at his friend intently for a moment, trying to take in the meaning of it all. Then he laid his hand on Paton's arm. "Missi, what can we do to help you now?"

Paton smiled to himself, thinking of how he could have used their help while digging the well. Now that the project was completed, they were eager to help.

"Well, chief, you know how the wall fell in once. I wish to put a ring of coral blocks all around the sides so it cannot fall in again. Let each man here go to the seashore and bring coral to line the wall."

Scarcely were the words out of Paton's mouth before the whole group of men rushed to the seashore, half a mile away. One by one they returned, each staggering under the largest block he could carry. Paton accepted them, chipped them into shape, then descended into the hole. As the blocks were lowered, he lined the wall with them. After the lining was twenty feet up from the bottom, Paton's hands were so badly cut from the jagged coral that he said he would have to rest for a week. But the chief would not listen to such an idea.

"Missi, we know you are tired, for you have worked hard. Now, you sit here and point to where the blocks are to go, and we will place them. No man sleeps tonight until this task is finished."

Wanting a share in what was happening, the women also brought coral blocks. Not satisfied with stopping at the top, they placed one row of blocks around the top to prevent children or animals from falling in.

The story of the well soon spread all over the island. Some of the men thought that they too would dig a well. But although later they dug five or six, they found only salt water.

"Missi dug, but he prayed also," explained the disappointed islanders. "We must learn to pray like Missi if we want to find fresh water."

From all over, men and women came to see the well and to drink of its water. Chief Namakei could scarcely bear to leave it. Then, thoughtfully, he said to Paton, "Missi, I think I could help you next Sabbath. Will you let me talk to my people about the well?"

Paton immediately consented. "Yes, by all means. If you will try to bring all the people to hear you."

Word spread like wildfire that Chief Namakei was to speak at the next worship service. When the time came there was present what was a great crowd for Aniwa. He appeared dressed in shirt and grass skirt. Mr. Paton conducted the sing-song and prayers. Then he invited Namakei to speak.

The old chief arose. "Friends of Namakei, men and women and children of Aniwa, listen to my words. The world is turned upside down since the word of Jehovah came to this island. Whoever expected to see rain coming up through the earth?"

He continued with words that touched the hearts of the people and brought tears to Paton's eyes.

"For years Missi has been telling us about a great God in heaven, and we did not believe him. He likewise told us that water could be found by digging into the earth, and we did not believe that either. We thought he had gone mad. But now look at the hole with the water in it. Missi's words have always been true.

"Something here in my heart tells me that the Jehovah

God, the Invisible One, does exist. This One, whom we never heard of till the Missi brought Him to our knowledge, I now believe in."

He then proposed that the people of Aniwa cease to worship gods that had never helped them, and worship instead the Jehovah God who had helped the missionary bring rain up from the ground.

His concluding words thrilled the audience:

"Let us burn and bury and destroy these things of wood and stone, and let us be taught by Missi how to serve the God who can hear, who sent His Son Jesus to die for us and bring us to heaven. This is what Missi has been telling us every day since he landed on Aniwa. We used to laugh at him, but now we believe him. The Jehovah God has sent us rain from the earth. Why should He not also send us His Son from heaven?

"Namakei stands up for Jehovah!"

Thus did a heathen chief, who in past years had partaken of cannibal feasts, lead his people to make their decision for Jesus. By digging that well, John Paton had indeed broken the back of heathenism on Aniwa.

THE CONQUEST OF ANIWA

THE Sunday afternoon following his sermon, Chief Namakei and several of his people came to Paton's house with their idols and threw them at John's feet.

"We no longer believe in these. We no longer worship them. We want to be done with them."

During the weeks that followed, company after company from various parts of the island came and piled their gods of wood and stone in heaps. Some threw theirs down with tears of relief that they were no longer superstitiously bound by them. Others shouted joyfully, "Jehovah! Jehovah!"

The wooden gods were piled together and burned. Others were buried in pits twelve or fifteen feet deep.

Some of the gods that had a particularly powerful hold on the people were loaded into canoes, paddled far out to sea, and thrown overboard, where they sank out of sight. Never again would they deceive the Aniwans.

Life for the Aniwanese changed remarkably as a result of their acceptance of Christianity. Crimes and quarrels were no longer settled by the club, but by rules agreed upon by the chiefs and their people. Property became safe. Previously, whenever anybody traveled about the island, he had to carry his valuables with him, or they would be stolen. Now they could be left at home.

The natives brought their gods and piled them up to be
burned. The gospel had won their hearts and minds.

The time now had come to build a new church. The hut originally used as a church was too small.

Paton explained the need to the people, making it clear that if it was agreed to build, no one would be paid; they would have to build it for the love of Jesus. All except one chief agreed that it was a good plan.

Enthusiastically, the people went to work. The women prepared sugar cane leaf for roof thatch, the men cut down suitable trees. Coral was heaped near the site of the new church, to be broken up small for the floor.

As the church went up, it was discovered that one more large tree was needed to complete an important part of the building. But even after a search of the whole island, none of the right size could be found.

One morning Paton was awakened by the sound of shouting and singing. Looking out the window, he saw the chief who had refused to cooperate, now with many of his men carrying a long log; it was the ridge-pole of his own house. The pole was blackened by the smoke of a thousand fires, but now he was offering it for the church. Many of the builders objected to using it; the other trees were white and clean. But Paton thanked him wholeheartedly for the gift. So it was hoisted in place, standing in stark contrast to the others. As long as the church remained, the old chief's gift served its useful purpose.

When the Patons had left Australia on their way to Aniwa, John had been presented with a silver communion service by the women of a Presbyterian church in Melbourne. Now —three years later—the time had come when it could be used. It was a memorable day indeed for John when he, his wife, and the new Christians partook together of the Lord's Supper. As he looked at those people whose hands had once been stained with the blood of cannibalism, reaching out to receive the emblems of the blood and body of their new Lord, he perhaps thought of the words of Paul, "I am not ashamed of the gospel of Christ: for it is the power of God unto salvation."

But Satan was by no means finished with Aniwa, and he continued to stir up trouble. One day as Paton was working near the church, Nourai, one of those who held onto his heathenism, rushed at John and began to strike at him with his musket. Paton managed to dodge the blows. Some men standing nearby were too surprised to do anything. Some women finally rescued Paton. They rushed up and pushed Nourai aside. The savage quickly disappeared into the bush.

This was a serious matter, and Paton called the Christians together to discuss it.

"You must stop this bad conduct," he said, "or I shall leave Aniwa and go to some island where my life will be protected."

Early the next morning about a hundred men gathered in front of the mission house. They were determined to go to Nourai's village and put an end to such bad conduct. They invited Paton to go with them. Since they were armed, he agreed to go, knowing that his intervention might be needed to prevent bloodshed.

On the outskirts of Nourai's village the culprit and his brother were spotted with guns in their hands, lurking at the edge of the public square. Some of Paton's friends rushed toward them, but they disappeared into the bush. Then the group went to the square to speak with the chief, the sacred man, and others.

A great debate followed, and the heathen were properly impressed by the emphatic words of Paton's companions. Finally one of Paton's special friends, Tai, stood up and said, "You think that Missi is here alone, and that you can do with him as you please! No! We are now all Missi men. We will fight for him rather than see him injured. Everyone who attacks him attacks us. That is settled today!"

The sacred man had pretended that he had brought hurricanes to the island, so in the general scolding he got a generous share. Paton's companions knew that he had a stiff knee. Surely, they said, with much laughter, a man able to create a hurricane could cure a sore knee. The more they laughed, the more sullen he became, but there was nothing he could do.

Suddenly his wife, a husky Malay woman, rushed up to him and scolded him for bringing all this trouble on their village. Becoming really indignant, she ran into the bush, grabbed a large coconut tree branch, and began to lash his shoulders, scolding him all the while and shouting, "I'll knock the tevil [devil] out of him. I'll do for him. He'll not try hurricanes again."

Paton remonstrated with her.

"I think you should stop now. See how quietly he takes it all! You don't want to kill him."

The sacred man solemnly promised to make no more hurricanes. Never again would he pretend to make people sick. After this success, Paton's companions marched triumphantly back to their homes. There was no more trouble of that nature again.

Once a year a general meeting of all Presbyterian Christian workers was held on one or another of the islands of the New Hebrides. One year, when the meetings were being held on Aneityum, Chief Namakei asked permission to go with the Patons. John did not want him to go, for by now the old chief was old and very frail. What if he should die away from Aniwa? But the chief and his family begged so hard that he finally agreed.

Before leaving Aniwa, Namakei called all his people together and bade them farewell. Whether he returned or not, he told them, they must always be strong for Jesus. Be loyal to the mission, he begged, and treat Missi kindly. When the old man boarded the ship his people stood on the shore weeping.

Namakei enjoyed every meeting. He was thrilled to learn that one island after another was being won for Jesus.

"Missi," he said after one inspiring session, "I am lifting up my head like a tree. I am growing tall with joy!"

Before the synod ended the old chief became sick. When Paton visited him, Namakei told his missionary that he did not expect to see Aniwa again. He wanted to send his love to his people and urge them to meet him in heaven.

"I am going," he said. "Missi, let me hear your words rising up in prayer, and then my heart will have strength to go. Oh, my Missi, my dear Missi, I go before you, but I will meet you again in the house of Jesus. Farewell."

And so old Namakei, Paton's first convert on Aniwa, died and was buried on Aneityum, where he waits the call of the One he had learned to love.

Litsi, Chief Namakei's daughter, had lived with the missionaries since the age of ten. Finally the time came for her to marry, and many young men sought her hand. But she held her head proudly and declared, "I am queen of my island, and when I like, I will ask a husband in marriage, as Missi told us the great Queen Victoria did!"

Finally she married a man named Mungaw. Mungaw, the son of a chief and heir to the chieftainship, was a strong Christian. He proved this one day when some men tried to pick a quarrel with him. They aimed their muskets at him as if to shoot.

"Don't call me a coward or think me afraid to die," he replied. "If I die now, I will go to be with Jesus. I am no longer a heathen. I am a Christian, and I wish to treat you as a Christian should."

The two men were eventually disarmed and, finally, they apologized for their actions.

Paton took his friend Mungaw along on one of his trips to Australia to show the churches what God's love could do for a heathen cannibal. Mungaw was an eloquent speaker and Paton interpreted for him in many of the churches in South Australia.

While they were visiting in Melbourne Mrs. Paton became very ill, and Mr. Paton had to remain with her. He took Mungaw to the railway station and asked a railway guard to see that he was put on a train going to St. Kilda where their temporary home was, and that he be put off there. Before the train came some white men saw Mungaw sitting in the station and lured him into a saloon. There they tried to get him to drink. When he refused they threw him on the floor and poured drugged whisky into him until he was half dead. Then they robbed him of all his money, about twelve dollars, leaving him with just one penny in his pocket.

Slowly he regained consciousness. It took him a few minutes to remember where he was. Staggering out onto the street, he heard a train whistle in the distance. He followed the sound to the station, where he tried to buy a ticket with his penny. Finally a sailor took pity on him, led him to an eating house, and bought him some food, then took him to the proper station for St. Kilda. Again he offered his penny for a ticket, only to be refused. In desperation he broke into the little English he knew.

"If me savvy (knew) road, me go. Me no savvy road, and stop here me die. My Missi Paton live at Kilda. Me want to go Kilda. Me no money. Bad fellow took all! Send me Kilda."

At last some good Samaritan bought Mungaw a ticket and put him on the right train. At the Paton house in St. Kilda, the poor fellow lay in a daze for nearly three weeks. From then on he was dreadfully changed. Never again could he tell his story in the churches. The Patons put him on a boat for Aniwa, and though he was happy to be home, he was never the same again.

"White man spoil my head!" he would say. Gradually he became worse, scarcely knowing what he was doing. One day he set fire to his own house and burned all his possessions. That was bad enough, but when he began burning down the houses of his neighbors, no one knew what to do with him. There was no insane asylum on Aniwa. Life became difficult for Litsi, his gentle wife.

One evening after holding family worship, Mungaw decided to go out of doors. He said that he felt very hot. His wife begged him not to go. She had heard voices and knew that an evil man from Tanna, who had threatened to shoot Mungaw, was lurking nearby.

"I am not afraid to die," he replied. "Life is a curse and a burden. The white man spoiled my head. Let me go and die quickly, if there is any chance."

As Mungaw stepped out of the house he was shot and killed instantly, falling back into Litsi's arms. He was buried near the church where he had first attended worship. All his friends came to the funeral. They would always remember the kind of man he had been in happier days.

The work of the missionaries was spreading in the New Hebrides, and with it the need for more and better transportation than was available. During a General Assembly of the Presbyterian Church, held in Victoria, Australia, it was voted that John go back to England and try to raise money for a steamer rather than a sailing boat. So, in 1884 Paton sailed for England. For a year and a half he traveled among the churches. In Bristol he visited the orphanages conducted by George Müller, that man of faith. When Müller donated fifty pounds for the new boat, Paton remonstrated. "I would far rather give you five hundred pounds for the orphans," he remarked.

Müller smiled. "God provides for His orphans. I am sure you need it all," he replied.

Paton's mission was very successful. Instead of the six thousand pounds he had set as his goal, he raised nine thousand.

John Paton and his wife returned to Aniwa once more for a visit. The whole island turned out to greet him. Describing the walk from the beach to the old house, John later wrote, "My procession to the old mission house was more like the triumphal march of a conqueror than that of a humble missionary." He found that the services he had started were kept up by native teachers. "Jesus has taken possession [of Aniwa], never again to quit those shores," he wrote.

Paton was now sixty-two years old, and the hardships he had gone through had left their mark upon him. But although he no longer enjoyed the strength of his youth, his heart rejoiced when he learned that teachers from Aniwa had succeeded in lighting the gospel torch on Tanna.

John was now appointed chairman of the highest body of the Presbyterian Church in the islands. In 1892 he began a world tour, which lasted two years, during which he visited the United States, Canada, and England. From England he sailed back to Australia, from where he later sailed to a number of islands of the South Seas on a missions survey. He rejoiced to see that everywhere the message of the gospel was making progress and miraculously changing the lives of thousands of men and women who, only a few years before, had been cannibals.

Mrs. Paton died in 1905. John continued preaching for another two years, almost up to the time of his death at the age of eighty-three. What a wonderful day it will be for the Patons when they, with Namuri and Aholam, Namakei and Nowar, Litsi and Mungaw, and all the other jewels gathered out of heathenism, will stand in triumph before the throne of God!

Brave Men to the Battle

Here is the story of the true church of Jesus—the Waldenses—branded as heretics and pursued relentless by the Papacy.

Cabin Boy to Advent Crusader

The story of Adventist co-founder Joseph Bates, who devoted the last 25 years of his life to keeping God's commandments.

Other Titles from TEACH Services, Inc.

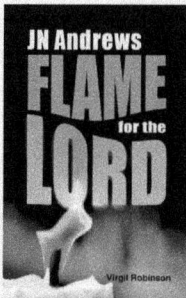

JN Andrews—Flame for the Lord

Virgil Robinson's account of J.N. Andrews—scholar, author, preacher, administrator and missionary.

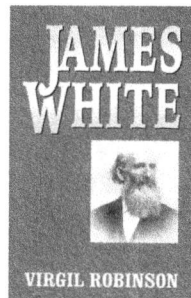

James White

Robinson's biography of Seventh-day Adventist church co-founder and preacher James White.

We invite you to view the complete
selection of titles we publish at:

www.TEACHServices.com

or write or email us your praises,
reactions, or thoughts about this
or any other book we publish at:

TEACH Services, Inc.
P U B L I S H I N G

www.TEACHServices.com

P.O. Box 954
Ringgold, GA 30736

info@TEACHServices.com

TEACH Services, Inc. titles may be purchased in bulk for
educational, business, fund-raising, or sales promotional use. For
information, please e-mail

BulkSales@TEACHServices.com.

Finally, if you are interested in seeing
your own book in print, please contact us at

publishing@teachservices.com.

We would be happy to review your manuscript for free.

www.ingramcontent.com/pod-product-compliance
Lightning Source LLC
Chambersburg PA
CBHW060542100426
42742CB00013B/2423